Archetypes and the Real You

Discover Your True Self, Unleash Your Superpowers, and Transform Your Life Through Archetype Psychology and Philosophy

© Copyright 2025 - All rights reserved.

The content contained within this book may not be reproduced, duplicated, or transmitted without direct written permission from the author or the publisher.

Under no circumstances will any blame or legal responsibility be held against the publisher or author for any damages, reparation, or monetary loss due to the information contained within this book, either directly or indirectly.

Legal Notice:

This book is copyright-protected. It is only for personal use. You cannot amend, distribute, sell, use, quote, or paraphrase any part of the content within this book without the consent of the author or publisher.

Disclaimer Notice:

Please note the information contained within this document is for educational and entertainment purposes only. All effort has been executed to present accurate, up-to-date, reliable, and complete information. No warranties of any kind are declared or implied. Readers acknowledge that the author is not engaging in the rendering of legal, financial, medical, or professional advice. The content within this book has been derived from various sources. Please consult a licensed professional before attempting any techniques outlined in this book.

By reading this document, the reader agrees that under no circumstances is the author responsible for any losses, direct or indirect, that are incurred as a result of the use of the information contained within this document, including, but not limited to, errors, omissions, or inaccuracies.

Your Free Gift
(only available for a limited time)

Thanks for getting this book! If you want to learn more about various spirituality topics, then join Mari Silva's community and get a free guided meditation MP3 for awakening your third eye. This guided meditation mp3 is designed to open and strengthen ones third eye so you can experience a higher state of consciousness. Simply visit the link below the image to get started.

https://spiritualityspot.com/meditation

Or, Scan the QR code!

Table of Contents

INTRODUCTION 1
CHAPTER 1: ARCHETYPES – THE PSYCHOLOGY BEHIND YOUR TRUE SELF 3
CHAPTER 2: THE PURE SOUL – GUARDIAN OF INNOCENCE 15
CHAPTER 3: THE SURVIVOR – MASTER OF RESILIENCE 23
CHAPTER 4: THE HERO – SEEKER OF QUESTS AND CHALLENGES 32
CHAPTER 5: THE NURTURER – HEALER OF SOULS 40
CHAPTER 6: THE EXPLORER – PURSUER OF NEW HORIZONS 48
CHAPTER 7: THE REBEL – CHALLENGER OF NORMS 56
CHAPTER 8: THE HEARTKEEPER – LOVER OF EMOTIONS 64
CHAPTER 9: THE VISIONARY – ARCHITECT OF THE FUTURE 72
CHAPTER 10: THE DISRUPTOR – WITTY INSTIGATOR OF TRANSFORMATION 80
CHAPTER 11: THE WISE ONE – KEEPER OF KNOWLEDGE 88
CONCLUSION 96
HERE'S ANOTHER BOOK BY MARI SILVA THAT YOU MIGHT LIKE 99
YOUR FREE GIFT (ONLY AVAILABLE FOR A LIMITED TIME) 100
REFERENCES 101
IMAGE SOURCES 104

Introduction

Discovering and truly understanding your authentic inner self is an essential life accomplishment that's overlooked all too often. Revealing your authentic self means understanding your weaknesses and also unveiling a whole spectrum of hidden strengths that you never knew existed within you. Only then will you be able to fully actualize and fulfill your true potential as an individual.

Self-discovery is often overlooked.[1]

Far from being a recent phenomenon, this pursuit of self-realization and understanding has occupied spiritually and philosophically curious people for millennia. More recently, however, fresh insights have come from various fields, particularly psychology. One popular framework focused on actualization is the Jungian concept of archetypes, formulated by the famous Swiss psychologist Carl Jung. The concept of archetypes is related to his wider concept of the collective unconscious that permeates all of humanity.

Understanding these archetypes means gaining insight into universal ideas and thinking patterns that exist in all human beings regardless of their cultural and linguistic background. Archetype psychology delves into the unconscious aspects of thinking and behavior on a global scale, and as a result, it reveals these things in the individual as well. As you study the archetypes, you'll discover both subtle and overt ways in which they influence your personality, choices, and your hidden potential. The ultimate goal of this self-searching endeavor is to unlock and activate your innate strengths and full potential.

While this book will explain the original concept of archetype psychology, it will also provide a unique take on the archetypes. This unique spin will go beyond traditional Jungian principles and the well-established works of successive authors, who have built upon Jungian psychology in later years.

With this vast body of psychological study as its foundation, this book will offer you theoretical insights and practical guidance through a unique set of ten archetypes. You'll receive a detailed yet highly palatable guide that will help you understand the archetypes and assimilate them into your everyday life.

The ten archetypes explored in this book have been carefully adapted and condensed to give you easy access to over a century of diligent research and philosophy by some of the greatest minds in the field of psychology. This format will ensure that, apart from theoretical knowledge, you'll receive plenty of actionable steps, tips, advice, and strategies. These practical insights will help you identify your most approximate archetypes, overcome their weaknesses, and effect real, positive changes in your life.

Chapter 1: Archetypes – The Psychology Behind Your True Self

In practical terms, putting archetypal psychology to good use in your life is all about studying each archetype carefully and identifying how much each of them manifests within you and in what way. This opening chapter will introduce you to the overall concept of archetypes, particularly in the way Carl Jung wrote and talked about them. You'll also learn a bit about how these archetypes play a role in psychology and how exactly they influence a person's identity.

Carl Jung.[1]

Archetypes 101

In the simplest terms, you can view the original Jungian archetypes as symbols or motifs that have persistently appeared across human civilizations. They show up in oral traditions, children's stories, dreams, literature, legends, myths, and much more. Some of the Jungian archetypes, which are often condensed into twelve distinct symbols, include things like the ruler, outlaw, hero, lover, jester, and others.

Anywhere you look across the world and throughout history, you'll find figures in human stories. This is because the archetypes are inherited, universal, and all belong to a collective unconscious that all humans share.

These archetypes can be seen as powerful influences on the thinking, behavior, and personalities of individuals. The archetypes can hold answers to your deepest impulses, strengths, weaknesses, desires, motivations, fears, and much more.

The message is that the archetypes aren't the aforementioned cultural motifs in a literal sense. These motifs are the *conscious* representations of the archetypes created by humans under the guidance of the invisible hand of the core archetypes, which exist in your *unconscious* mind, yet are always at work.

The archetypes are foundational aspects of the human psyche, and their influence isn't readily observable. The results of their influence, however, comprise the entirety of human behavior, emotions, and meaning and, therefore, are quite clear. In a way, the archetypes are everywhere, and they are everything.

The standardized twelve archetypes that you'll usually encounter represent a condensed and more digestible version of the intricate philosophies of Carl Jung. Jung himself drew on his psychological expertise – but also on ancient Greek philosophy, going all the way back to Plato. The likes of James Hillman contributed their own interpretations in the 20th century and consolidated the concept for use in psychology and its numerous branches.

Jung drew ideas from as far back as Plato.[a]

Carl Jung spoke of archetypes as unconscious, inherited predispositions or behavioral traits and tendencies that differ from instincts. As an instigator of the concept, he is considered a founder of original archetypal psychology, whereas psychologists like Hillman helped push this field in a certain direction and bring it closer to the mainstream.

The Role of Archetypes in Modern Psychology

Psychologists who make use of archetypes in their practice tend to consider them as a sort of map or blueprint for human psychology in the broadest sense. Psychological practices are a major topic in their own right, but the basic understanding of archetypes, in this context, would be their use in discovering the complex universal patterns of human behavior and thinking.

With this view as a foundation, a psychologist might use archetypes to observe how these universal patterns manifest in an individual human being. This means deciphering certain predispositions and traits that produce deep motivations, fears, desires, inclinations, and much more. More importantly, in the practical sense, the archetypes can help psychologists and therapists understand where a person is coming from and empathize with them on a deeper level. Through this understanding, individuals can begin their healing processes, embark on a journey of self-discovery, and fulfill their potential.

Archetypal psychology generally posits that every individual harbors a range of archetypal influences in their psyche. There can be as few or as many such forces at work as an individual's personal disposition allows. Knowing how these forces operate and recognizing them in people unlocks the doorway toward understanding how thoughts, emotions, and behaviors are shaped.

In everyday psychology and for you as a regular person, archetypes are a pathway into your and other people`s psyche. If self-discovery is a difficult task for you, it's always a good idea to start by observing the influence of archetypes in others. Learning about archetypes and looking for them in people will help you understand their behavior and mental states with more depth.

This is a good way to foster empathy, and the more you see these archetypal patterns in other people and yourself, the less judgmental you'll be. The bottom line is that the practical application of archetypal psychology is all about understanding the intricacies of personality without the cloud of judgment or frustration. This becomes easier when you observe behaviors, thoughts, and feelings through the lens of archetypes because they provide answers and context to everything you observe. All of these things belong to the same unconscious collective that all humans are a part of.

How Archetypes Influence Identity

The nucleus of Jung's view on the archetypes was the contemplation of four major archetypes. His philosophy developed further from there, and he believed that the potential number of different archetypes was functionally limitless. Baseline archetypes could intertwine and work together in various combinations, leading to the rise of entirely new archetypes. The four essential archetypes include the persona, shadow, anima/animus, and self.

1. Persona

Your persona archetype is all about the image of yourself that you project to the outside world. While it's derived from the Latin word for "mask," your persona acts more as a protective shield than a deceptive cover. People will behave differently in different groups and settings – an instinctive and natural way of protecting the ego. In the broadest sense, your persona consists of all the behaviors you were taught from childhood.

The persona is a containment field that keeps primordial urges and instincts in check and helps you function as a member of a community. In practical terms, the persona is also about adaptability to environments and all the ways in which they shape you. This refers to the influence of your family, local community, nation, culture, and all the other external factors that shape you. The trick is to make sure that the persona doesn't take over completely and suppress your authentic inner self, which all humans possess within them.

2. Shadow

Your shadow archetype has sexual and instinctual dimensions, referring to all the unconscious things within you. The shadow also correlates with the repressed. These repressed contents of your mind and character include weaknesses, deep desires, ideas, and many other things. Usually, these are things that conflict with your own morals and those of wider society and its norms. As such, the shadow has an obvious dark connotation and refers to the darkness that lurks in every human being to some degree. The key to dealing with the shadow is to understand it and embrace it as a natural, wild element of humanity that can be kept inside without being acted upon. Refusing to acknowledge the shadow can allow it to take over or be projected on other people out of frustration.

3. Anima

Respectively, the anima and the animus describe the feminine and masculine sides of the psyche that exist in individuals of the opposite sex. Every man and woman possesses the anima or animus on some level, allowing them to channel the best of both worlds within their conduct. As always, balance is essential, and the rejection of this opposite sex in the unconscious mind can lead to missteps in the way a person relates to their own sex or that of others.

Jung saw the anima and animus as essential channels of communication between the individual and the collective unconscious. Individuals will naturally suppress their anima or animus to an extent, but the key is to find ways to harness these archetypes. Jung believed that each individual should explore both their feminine and masculine sides to some extent. He associated the anima with empathy, intuition, emotions, and trust, while the animus represents logic, stability, and problem-solving. From there, it's easy to see how the feminine and masculine aspects of humanity come together to form any healthy and functional individual. There can simply be no wholeness in an individual who doesn't cherish, explore, and develop both aspects of their psyche.

4. Self

Last but not least, Jung described the archetype of the self. The self consists of all of your characteristics on the conscious and unconscious levels, coming together to form one whole – which is you. Jung posited that a conflict between the conscious and unconscious – if it exists – must be resolved in every person. Discord between these two aspects of the self will ultimately lead to emotional and psychological issues. Reconciling the two is all about creating a holistic self and achieving a level of personal cohesion through a process known as individuation.

Per Jung, the overlapping and interaction of these four core archetypes creates an endless array of more specific archetypes. Among them, the twelve most discussed archetypes include the ruler, creator (artist), sage, innocent, explorer, rebel (outlaw), hero (warrior), magician (wizard), jester (trickster), everyman, lover, and caregiver. These and many other archetypes emerge in every person as a result of the unique ways in which their four primary archetypes interact with each other. You'll identify aspects of all of these and other archetypes in the ten special archetypes devised for this book, learning how each of them plays a part in your identity and how they can be harnessed.

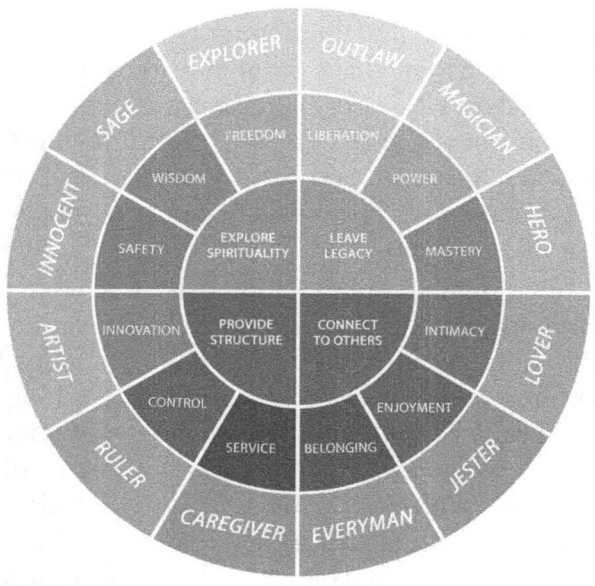

Overview of Archetypes in the Book

As mentioned earlier, this book will provide its own list of ten archetypes. These archetypes will be unique in that they won't correspond exactly to Jung's categories, but they will certainly contain all of his insights and those from other famous psychologists who have delved into this topic. Some of the archetypes in the book are directly based on a specific Jungian archetype, while others will draw influence from multiple traditional archetypes and combine their characteristics for a more comprehensive view of their influences and traits. The archetypes you'll explore include the following:

- **The Pure Soul** – *Guardian of Innocence:* The Pure Soul is influenced by Jungian archetypes, such as the child and the innocent. This archetype is inherently optimistic, warm, and open-minded. It is regarded as an archetype with an uncorrupted heart that's prone to idealism and possesses an overarching trust in people and goodness.

- **The Survivor** – *Master of Resilience:* This archetype is all about strength, endurance in adversity, and mental or emotional fortitude. The Survivor can persevere through any challenge through sheer will.

- **The Hero** – *Seeker of Quests and Challenges:* The Hero shares a few similarities with the Survivor, but also exhibits an inherent ability to lead. The Hero loves a challenge and is the embodiment of ambition and courage, possessing unrelenting drive and purpose in their actions.

- **The Nurturer** – *Healer of Souls:* The Nurturer is a generous soul and a hopeless empath who possesses a deep understanding of other people and a strong desire to help them through selfless action.

- **The Explorer** – *Pursuer of New Horizons:* The Explorer is an incurable adventurer who loves venturing into the unknown. This archetype is oriented toward accumulating new experiences and making discoveries.

- **The Rebel** – *Challenger of Norms:* The Rebel lives to challenge established conventions, ask questions, and speak truth to power. This defiant archetype thrives on change and is characterized by courage, boldness, and a thirst for freedom. The Rebel correlates with Jung's outlaw archetype.

- **The Heartkeeper** – *Lover of Emotions:* The Heartkeeper embodies passion in all its forms. This is an empathetic, emotionally sophisticated archetype capable of forming unbreakable bonds with other people and is a frequent source of unconditional love.

- **The Visionary** – *Architect of the Future:* The Visionary excels at planning and is usually pronounced in people who are inventors and innovators. A person dominated by this archetype sees the limits of what's possible as opportunities for new breakthroughs. Creativity and imagination are the Visionary's strongest points.

- **The Disruptor** – *Witty Instigator of Transformation:* Based on Jung's trickster archetype, the Disruptor is somewhat similar to the Rebel. The biggest differences are the Disruptor's wit, humor, and cleverness. People influenced by this archetype can poke fun at almost anything and are markedly playful. They often instigate controversy and provoke others as a means of motivating change and transformation.

- **The Wise One** – *Keeper of Knowledge:* Most similar to Jung's sage, the Wise One is an archetype that's all about wisdom, learning, and mentorship. This archetype produces excellent advisors who live to guide others while also constantly expanding their own wealth of knowledge.

Being More Than One Archetype

All of these archetypes come together to influence the holistic image of humanity's collective unconscious. On an individual level, however, human beings can be quite different from each other. Depending on your inherent characteristics and the way you were brought up, you might have very strong personal definitions. This could result in a powerful, dominant influence of just one archetype.

For instance, a person who is an avid bookworm with little interest in anything other than reading and studying is clearly under the spell of the Wise One. On the other hand, a trope, such as the warrior poet, would serve as an example of a person dominated by more than one archetype.

It's completely normal for a person to embody two or even more archetypes at the same time.

In fact, individuals whose identity draws on just one archetype are something of a rarity. Humans are complex creatures that often harbor a variety of interests and skills, and most people will derive life fulfillment and enjoyment from numerous sources. Being influenced by more than one archetype can also sometimes result in internal conflict, but more often than not, your archetypes will work in unison to paint the picture of who you are as a person.

Indeed, understanding the archetypes isn't just about self-discovery and information. It's also about reconciliation between different aspects of your personality and about balance, which will help you make sure that all of your strengths are allowed to shine with equal glow. Hopefully, This chapter has allowed you to gain some initial insight into which archetypes resonate with you the most while also illustrating that every archetype is equally important for humanity as a whole. Each of them represents a different facet of the human experience in this life, complementing each other and demonstrating the wide scope of human pursuit and ways of being.

Quick Archetypes Quiz

Before you delve deeper into each of the archetypes described in this book, you might want to take a basic quiz to establish some points of reference. This will give you something to compare and analyze against as you learn about each archetype and try to identify which of them you relate to the most. After you've read this book, you are encouraged to conduct an online search for more detailed tests, including the ones focused specifically on Jungian archetypes.

The six questions below will feature multiple answers that correlate with different archetypes, which you'll find in the following chapters in their respective order. Mark a single point for each of your answers, and when you're done, your most dominant archetype will have the most points. More than one archetype can end up having multiple points, which is natural because several archetypes can influence each individual.

Keep a record of your answers as you progress through the rest of the book. As you learn about the archetypes, it will become clear how your answers are reflected in each one of them. If there is no clear winner among the archetypes, you can try giving more than one answer to the questions, wherever applicable. This should at least provide you with a ranking order of their presence and influence in your psyche.

1. **How do you typically react to challenges?**
   a. You immediately visualize a positive outcome and easily focus on it.
   b. You feel the utmost stability and conviction in your ability to adapt, overcome, and improvise to meet any challenge.
   c. You welcome the opportunity with confidence and a powerful drive to succeed.
   d. No challenge is too great if someone needs your help.
   e. You see it as an adventure and an opportunity for self-discovery and growth.
   f. You're open to change and are inclined to think outside the box, which you'll leverage when facing a challenge.
   g. Your passion enables you to take on most challenges, but emotions can get in the way at times.
   h. Your inventiveness and ability to think way ahead make you confident no matter the challenge you face.
   i. You have a way of being clever and innovative with provocative solutions, but challenges can become difficult when you don't take them seriously.
   j. You see challenges as an opportunity for learning and tend to approach them by observing and understanding the bigger picture with calculation, clarity of thought, and planning.

2. **How do you deal with failures and setbacks?**
   a. You'll find it easy to maintain a positive attitude and retain a firm belief in a good outcome.
   b. Unshaken by failure, you promptly think of new solutions to any problem, even if it means a radical change in direction.
   c. You remain goal-oriented and welcome the challenge with confidence.
   d. You'll persevere in the service of others, but the feeling of failure can be powerful if it results in harm to others.
   e. You embrace hardship as a learning opportunity and welcome the new experience.

f. You tend to challenge conventional thinking and aren't reluctant to carve a new pathway if previous attempts fail.
g. As a passionate and emotional individual, you might feel drained, but your strong relationships provide a support structure.
h. When the going gets tough, you have a way of inventing novel approaches and dictating the reality of the situation through sheer vision, but frustration is also a possibility.
i. On an emotional level, you cope with failure very effectively through wit and humor.
j. Temporary setbacks are unlikely to shake you up because you can usually see beyond the immediate, never losing sight of the wider plan and ultimate goal.

3. **Which of these things brings you the most fulfillment?**
a. Pursuing goodness in all things and upholding your ideals.
b. Overcoming obstacles, solving problems, and staying strong.
c. Pushing boundaries, pursuing your goals, and coming out on top in any challenge.
d. Helping people in whatever way is needed.
e. Exploration, adventure, and diving into the unknown.
f. Challenging the status quo and breaking conventions.
g. Fostering deep emotional bonds with people and exploring all things related to feelings.
h. Identifying opportunities, innovating, inventing, and being consumed by ideas and imagination until that which you envision comes to fruition.
i. Kicking up a fuss by being cleverly and humorously provocative, pushing boundaries, and disrupting conventions.
j. The chase for knowledge, understanding, and wisdom, as well as imparting that wisdom to others and being the advisor.

4. **Which of these things comes most naturally to you?**
a. Believing in the inherent goodness of people and life as a whole.
b. Pressing on through adversity and staying stable.
c. Being ambitious, driven, and a leader.
d. Empathy, compassion, and supportiveness.
e. Treading into unfamiliar territory and leaving your comfort zone.

f. Questioning authority and defying oppressive constraints in all their forms.
g. Getting passionate about something, especially people or goals you deeply care about.
h. Creativity, foresight, innovation, and imagination.
i. Being playful and lighthearted in virtually any situation.
j. Reading, reflecting, contemplating, and advising others.

5. Which of these compliments do you get most often?

a. You're optimistic, open-minded, and have a pure heart.
b. You're strong, resilient, and persistent.
c. You're courageous, ambitious, and inspiring.
d. You're a great listener, a supportive person, and a great help.
e. You're bold, adventurous, and very independent.
f. You have a critical mind and are a free thinker.
g. You're a devoted person with great emotional depth and are filled with love.
h. You're creative, clever, and possess a keen mind for innovation.
i. You're witty, funny, clever, and purposefully provocative.
j. You're patient, thoughtful, and present wisdom beyond your years.

6. Which of these criticisms do you often receive?

a. You're naive and too trusting.
b. You're unfeeling, and don't allow yourself to be vulnerable.
c. You're overconfident and push yourself too hard.
d. You're too hard on yourself or prone to self-neglect.
e. You have a tendency to be restless and unwilling to commit.
f. You can be impulsive, hardheaded, and even reckless.
g. You can be too emotional at times or even possessive.
h. You might be too consumed by dreams and visions at times, leading you to unrealistic thinking.
i. You sometimes provoke without purpose and can be irresponsible or even cynical.
j. You can be too analytical and prone to wandering off in your thoughts, as well as unemotional.

Chapter 2: The Pure Soul – Guardian of Innocence

The archetype referred to here as the Pure Soul is a powerful archetype that can be a tremendous positive force in your life if its influence takes hold.

It draws influence from Jung's archetypes, such as the innocent and the child, and also a sub-archetype that Caroline Myss refers to as the divine child. If properly harnessed, this archetype can infuse your life with childlike wonder, optimism, and general goodness.

The Divine Child.'

Archetype Profile

The key traits that define the Pure Soul include things like optimism, idealism, and a trusting attitude toward life and all that it brings, which includes the people that the Pure Soul meets.

Right off the bat, it's clear that this archetype can be an enriching influence in your life, but it also has its pitfalls. Indeed, one of the things you'll quickly realize as you explore the ten archetypes in the upcoming chapters is that each of them has a potentially negative side. This can be referred to as the archetype's shadow side, and it can come to the forefront when it's underestimated or not appropriately integrated.

In its healthy form, the Pure Soul archetype will drive you to pursue and find joy everywhere you go in life and help you build a harmonious existence. Above the nuances of this archetype's traits, the overall picture is one of happiness and contentment. Optimism is just one source of this happiness. The Pure Soul's happiness also comes from seeing the best in people and always believing that everyone else possesses an inherent goodness.

This innocent outlook on other people allows the Pure Soul to experience little to no frustration, even when they are faced with some of the darker aspects of human behavior. When they are slighted by someone, Pure Souls will always find a way to explain it through some form of rationalization and retain their belief in goodness. This doesn't mean that the archetype necessarily lacks dignity or self-respect. A well-balanced Pure Soul isn't blind to evil but chooses to understand it instead of fearing it. Coupled with the firm belief that goodness can always prevail, it's plain to see how this archetype fuels its optimism.

The Pure Soul's trust in all that is good, in combination with their lust for life, can lead them down a path of intense idealism. It's not uncommon for people under this archetype to become active in pursuit of justice, although they are more likely to focus on just helping people instead of fighting things out with the opposition.

In keeping with its pure heart, this archetype is also characterized by sincerity and honesty. This honesty is an integral part of the Pure Soul's trusting nature, so they're also not reluctant to open up to others. The Pure Soul will generally assume good faith on the part of others, and they're easy to communicate with at a level of mutual respect and appreciation.

For all of these traits, individuals with a pronounced Pure Soul archetype tend to be a very positive influence on others. They're the kind of person who can lift the mood and enhance everyone's motivation. The Pure Soul is pleasant to be around and is trustworthy, making them a great asset in teams and communities of all kinds. Even though they're not highlighted for their mental fortitude, Pure Souls exhibit plenty of it in practice. Their positive outlook on life and other people allows them to keep a cool head and approach people and situations with understanding, openness, and kindness.

The Pure Soul is trustworthy and pleasant to be around.[4]

Embodying Innocence

Unless they experience a crushing disappointment that they can't process, Pure Souls are always cheerful and fulfilled. This is partly because they're so easy to impress. In balanced individuals, this apparent simplicity comes from a place of excitement about life, not frivolity. The Pure Soul is simple, genuine, and uncomplicated in all the best ways a person can be, but that doesn't have to entail ignorance or naivety.

As the Guardian of Innocence, this archetype views the world with the innocent eyes of a child. That means having little to no judgment or preconceptions, especially about people. As a general rule, the more suspicious and generalized notions you have when it comes to dealing with people, the less innocence there is in your outlook. Such considerations are natural and a necessary part of life that comes from experience, but the Pure Soul will never let caution or healthy skepticism diminish their ability to see the good in people.

This non-judgmental perception, often accompanied by fascination and interest, can give you a fresh perspective on many aspects of life. To apply the positive attributes of the Pure Soul in your daily life, you have to allow yourself to be vulnerable toward people and excited for life. For many people, that's easier said than done, but if you make an effort toward an attitude adjustment, you, too, can foster this archetype. That adjustment will have a mental dimension, but you can also encourage it through activities and practical changes, as you'll learn later in this chapter.

The key to embodying this archetype is to open up. That doesn't mean trusting people in situations where your common sense clearly tells you that you shouldn't, and it doesn't entail recklessness in the pursuit of happiness and fulfillment. It just means loosening your valves a little bit as a start – and trying to see what positive changes might emerge in your life as a result.

Seeing the silver lining in each cloud is an intrinsic attribute of the Pure Soul, but it can also be a skill to master. Misguided optimism and negativity bias are both equally uncritical, so a good place to start is trying to analyze situations more objectively and practice critical thinking. When faced with a difficult problem or a major setback, simply acknowledging how it's *not* an irreversible disaster can be a major leap toward a more positive attitude. As a start, try to at least be neutral in your assessments of people and situations so that you can get comfortable with *not* rushing to overwhelming negativity. Over time, this will give you more room to ponder the positives as well, and after a while, you might find that you're increasingly focusing on that side of the equation.

The Shadow of Vulnerability

The Pure Soul's greatest strengths and all those wonderful things that make this archetype so sympathetic can become its downfall if unchecked. It's simple enough to imagine a number of ways that individuals with this archetype can be vulnerable to malicious actors. The Pure Soul has a lot of trust in people, but the archetype can often lack the calculating, analytical, and discerning characteristics found in other archetypes.

This opens them up to deception and manipulation. The shadow Pure Soul is naive and vulnerable, which exposes them not just to harm but also to disillusionment if that harm does come. With happiness and joy being some of their main goals, Pure Souls can fall into disappointment and great despair if something happens that can shake up their belief in good outcomes. This archetype's optimism is strong, but it's not indestructible. A well-rounded Pure Soul must guard their optimism with common sense, self-care, and a healthy amount of caution.

The harsh realities of the world, especially if they aren't understood and planned for, can bring anybody down, and the Pure Soul is no exception. This can be especially troublesome for Pure Souls, who indulge in great idealism. If a Pure Soul neglects knowledge and realism, they can be just as easily disappointed as they are impressed. This archetype's strong association with the innocent nature of a child illustrates that their disappointment can be quite dramatic and overwhelming.

Apart from disappointment and pain, the Pure Soul's descent into the shadow realm can also manifest in denial. They can ignore the complexity of the issues they face, disregard legitimate concerns, and simply pursue their childishly positive vision of situations and people, which is usually a recipe for disaster. Denial can also make the Pure Soul resistant to change, convincing them that everything is going smoothly when, in fact, major problems demand their attention.

To avoid these pitfalls as a Pure Soul archetype, you must learn to use at least some objectivity when looking at yourself and your situation. Working on your critical thinking skills, becoming more analytical, and combining these things with self-respect can go a long way toward avoiding toxic relationships and grand disappointments. It's perfectly healthy to assume that people mean well as long as you are simply giving them the benefit of the doubt instead of blindly diving headfirst into their schemes.

The key is to maintain the awareness that trust should not be absolute and unconditional and that your benefit of the doubt is something that you willingly grant, not something that you owe. Beginning every interaction with courtesy and respect is commendable and entirely correct, but from that point on, continued respect must be earned through reciprocation.

Apart from identifying and avoiding bad actors, the Pure Soul must also learn how to avoid general disappointment with life and the world as a whole. Unfortunately, some Pure Souls have a tendency to neglect learning from exposure to negativity. Most people have a natural urge to bury their heads in the sand, but the occasional dose of reality is healthy and necessary if you are to remain grounded. The Pure Soul will have no problem finding beauty and focusing on it, even if they occasionally learn a thing or two about the darker side of things.

Indeed, an overwhelming insistence on positivity at all times is a common folly of the Pure Soul. Not only does this leave them vulnerable to disappointment, but it can also rub off on their relationships in a rather negative way. The shadow Pure Soul can thus disregard people's concerns and even become obtuse in their pursuit of joy and happiness, always eager to brush uncomfortable realities aside.

The Superpower of Vulnerability and Optimism

As is usually the case with archetypes, the Pure Soul's strengths are often the same things that can become weaknesses if they aren't in balance. The Pure Soul's optimism is a strength that can be so pronounced that it becomes akin to a superpower. Individuals dominated by the Pure Soul are capable of seeing a silver lining in virtually anything that life throws at them. It can be argued that this optimism is the archetype's greatest strength by far.

Some other archetypes take the spotlight when it comes to resilience, but the power of optimism is a potent tool of survival that makes the Pure Soul an underrated archetype in the resilience league. Pure Souls are known for their kindness, so their subtle form of strength goes underappreciated. In reality, this archetype can bounce back from failures and setbacks through the sheer force of will and thought, which epitomizes strength quite well.

To harness this kind of strength in your daily life, you should try to find ideals to believe in, activities to enjoy, and, most importantly, people you can trust. Every good person you can find in life will elevate your optimism and faith on an unconscious level. You might not develop an idealistic worldview overnight, but little by little, you can at least learn to keep your negativity and disappointment at bay. There is no switch to instantly attain the superpower of unwavering optimism. You simply have to make a deliberate effort to seek out the goodness in people and the world and embrace it to provide evidence for a belief in positive outcomes. This is especially important if you possess an analytical mind that thrives on being critical.

The sad truth is that people can get comfortable with negativity and cynicism due to inertia. At that point, it won't even occur to them that they've purposely exposed themselves exclusively to negative influences just to maintain that comfort or confirm their bias. If you have to see it to believe it, then you have to look for it, and if you actively look for goodness, you'll eventually find it. This isn't as much an optimistic hope as it is a statistical reality.

Harnessing the Inner Child

Fostering and harnessing the Pure Soul within you is largely an introspective exercise in that it requires reflection and mindfulness of the way you think about life. On the other hand, there are certainly many practical actions you can take to try and motivate your Pure Soul archetype to come to the forefront and take on a more active role in your life. This can be done through the settings you put yourself in or the people you interact with.

There will be moments where you experience childlike wonder.⁶

To start with, you'll find that keeping a journal can help you get in touch with the Pure Soul within you, as with a number of other archetypes. Journaling about this particular archetype would revolve around noting moments that make this archetype tingle or at least inspire you to reflect on its potential influence. These can be moments in which you experience childlike wonder or feel like you're getting in touch with how you used to be as a child.

A journal entry about such a moment would include a description of what happened and a detailed recounting of how it made you feel. The latter is essential because analyzing your feelings and thoughts will play a major part in helping you get in touch with any archetype, especially one that's known to be emotional. By exploring these feelings, you will be engaging in introspection, which is a key tool in self-discovery.

If the influence of the Pure Soul is seldom felt for you and you rarely find yourself enjoying the little moments or being stimulated by life, you can try and seek those moments out. Since this archetype is closely associated with Jung's child archetype, you can stimulate it by engaging in activities that remind you of your childhood or seeking out adventures, no matter how small they might be. Anything that helps you decontaminate your mind, decompress emotionally, and nourish your sense of purity is a good idea.

Spending time in nature, away from all the stresses and distractions of modern living, can be a great way to develop your ability to appreciate the present moment and all the little things it brings. Seeing new places, going hiking, and other ways of spending quality time outdoors can be incredibly stimulating for your senses and mental and emotional states. Even the most pessimistic and inert people can hardly stay indifferent in the face of a great mountain view or the ambiance of a lush forest in spring.

As a human being, you have a natural inclination for natural environments, which the constraints of urban living can repress. This lack of contact with the natural world and the sensory overload of urban life can lead to a subtle numbness that can make you disinterested and difficult to stimulate. This is only one of the ways in which people can lose their sense of childlike wonder and even their ability to enjoy life. New scenery, positive people, and hobbies can help you reignite that flame and start getting excited about things again.

Chapter 3: The Survivor – Master of Resilience

The Survivor is an amalgam of a couple of different Jungian and other archetypes, exhibiting characteristics that make it a naturally resilient archetype. This resilience is primarily mental and emotional, and it's quite often inherent in the archetype. Depending on your life circumstances, the Survivor can be one of the most desirable archetypes to have, but as with any archetype, the Survivor must be properly understood and kept in balance. This chapter will acquaint you with a powerful archetype that can enable individuals to weather almost any storm and how you might harness its power.

The Survivor.⁷

Archetype Profile

The Survivor can also be called the Master of Resilience because this archetype has a way of retaining composure in any situation and steadfastness in the face of adversity. This archetype is the image of strength, endurance, and perseverance, allowing certain people to endure stresses and setbacks in situations that could throw other people off balance. This strength is a powerful and useful trait, but it can incur costs in the realm of emotions and openness if permitted.

Unlike the Pure Soul, the Survivor might not always be concerned with the beauty of the world or pursue wonder and happiness, but they will know how to avert disappointment where the Pure Soul might struggle to stay the course. It's not that a balanced, rational Survivor archetype will seek out adversity, but they do tend to thrive in it. This isn't a question of deriving enjoyment from struggle for the sake of struggle, though. The Survivor simply feels comfortable taking on challenges and overcoming obstacles, with very little emotion involved in the process.

Part of this archetype's resilience comes from emotional invulnerability and adaptability to a range of situations. The survivors are usually confident and self-sufficient, have faith in their abilities, and understand that every problem has a solution. This archetype shares some key similarities with the Jungian "warrior," which means that they don't shy away from conflict if they deem it inevitable or reasonable. Needless to say, the Survivor's relationship with adversity must be kept in check so that the outcomes remain constructive and positive instead of destructive.

As a self-reliant archetype, the Survivor is unlikely to ask for help even when the situation warrants it. They don't mind keeping to themselves and solving their problems in silence, rarely expressing a need to vent their emotions or decompress. People guided by this archetype might not always exhibit an ambitious nature, but they certainly possess drive when they set their minds on a goal. In fact, their resistance to stress and pain offsets a need to be overly driven and energetic in their pursuits. The Survivor is the kind of person who doesn't have to achieve their goal in the shortest time possible, being content to work toward their objective in silence and patience.

When combined with other archetypes, however, the Survivor can be an unstoppable force to be reckoned with. If they can harness the ambition, confidence, and leadership of some of the other archetypes, Survivors can simply dominate every task in every setting. Overall, the Survivor can be relentless without being outwardly intense, loud, or grandiose in any way. The archetype's talent is in their ability to take punches and keep pressing on.

Embodying Endurance and Resilience

Embodying endurance and resilience boils down to analyzing your failures and problems in a level-headed manner and subtracting any notion of finality. Whether conscious or unconscious, a fatalist attitude is usually what leads to collapse in the face of adversity. The Survivor tackles their problems as they come and interprets them as momentary setbacks within a continuity of effort. Where a less resilient person might see an unsalvageable catastrophe, the Survivor finds new solutions or, when all else fails, life lessons. In that regard, resilience is all about what you choose to focus on when you encounter a roadblock.

The Survivor doesn't dwell on failure for the sake of dwelling, and they don't wallow in self-pity or self-flagellation. As such, this archetype understands the essential difference between dwelling and learning. The Survivor's resilience doesn't mean they always win in the end. A rational person ruled by this archetype will be realistic in their assessments and know when to cut their losses.

The trick is in how they process these losses on an emotional level and what their effects are on the archetype's long-term planning. The Survivor can entirely abandon a certain path if the going gets objectively impossible, but they'll do so without self-doubt, emotional damage, or a diminished self-image. After gathering what they've learned from a setback, Survivors will persist toward their long-term goal undeterred, only they might formulate an entirely new path.

If endurance is something you struggle with in your daily life, the good news is that each person has the capacity to improve their resilience. If you often find yourself faltering in times of adversity, you don't necessarily have to start moving mountains right away. You can start with tiny steps that will help you merely get in touch with your inner Survivor. Once you make contact and feel even a modicum of strength for the first time, it'll be much easier to take the next step.

For the moment, forget any of the professional failures you might have had or your emotional baggage. Start by thinking of all those minor, insignificant things that bring you down or irritate you on a daily basis, including all the moments in which you lose your cool or get the least bit frustrated. Succumbing to the stresses and pressures of regular life is death by a thousand cuts. If you can't be resilient in a traffic jam, you'll certainly have to work your way up until you reach a point where you'll tackle life's major obstacles confidently and calmly.

To be resilient is to be in charge of your thoughts and emotions. It's about having a choice and choosing to focus on opportunities, lessons, and long-term goals instead of the negative aspects of the here and now. On the other hand, resilience is not about being emotionless. Everyone gets frustrated or disappointed sometimes, but the resilient individual will know how to articulate those feelings and turn every situation constructively.

The Shadow of Hardiness

Seeing as strength itself is the defining characteristic of the Survivor, it's easy to overlook the ways in which this archetype can succumb to weaknesses. Somewhat counter-intuitively, the very strength of the Survivor can become its weak point if it's allowed to take over a person's life and suppress other positive traits that don't revolve around resilience.

Feeling and addressing your emotions is essential for any functional human being, and it'll reflect on your relationships, among other things. The Survivor's greatest challenges include emotional numbness, fear of vulnerability or weakness, and an overall hardened outlook. The Survivor, whose method of dealing with adversity boils down to suppressing their feelings, will eventually lose their ability to understand the feelings of others as well. Thick skin can be an invaluable shield, but it can also become a prison once this archetype forgets how to let the right influences in.

The Survivor who's been hurt is usually at the highest risk of completely shutting off. Being cold, distant, and ruthless might lead to a degree of material success if you're lucky, but it predictably becomes an isolating experience. The key is to maintain your resilience as a tool for constructive decision-making and problem-solving, not an emotional shield. Once resilience turns into a mere defense mechanism, the Survivor's shadow side will inevitably emerge.

A hurt Survivor usually becomes cold and distant.'

The easiest way to make sure that this isn't happening to you is to analyze when your emotional and mental shields tend to come up. If the shields are raised only when you're faced with a true setback or some kind of problem, then your Survivor archetype is likely healthy. However, if you feel shielded and numb when interacting with people and you feel that there is an emotional distance by default, then the shadow might be cast. This is most reflected in the way you communicate.

A resilient person who doesn't fear vulnerability won't clam up whenever they have to talk about themselves in any meaningful way. They'll process insults and attacks with stability and confidence when they happen, but they won't assume ill will by default and push everyone away just in case. They'll also be in touch with their own emotions and nourish their natural ability to empathize with the perspectives of others.

If you feel that you're too closed off, the best way to re-engage with life in a healthier way is to take baby steps beyond your comfort zone in whatever way is pertinent to your life. Meeting new people, opening up more personal topics with the people you already know, or pursuing novel experiences can all be great ways to do this. You must remember that resilience is not the avoidance of pain. It's the ability to be open to the world without the fear of failure and knowing how to emotionally process that failure and what it teaches – if it eventually happens.

Stability and Strength

Resilience, emotional fortitude, mental stability, adaptability, and relentlessness are all key strengths of the Survivor. If there's one key strength that all of these traits share, it could be summarized as mental clarity. The ability to think clearly and drown out the unconscious noise that might cloud the minds of other people when they're having a hard time is the Survivor's superpower.

This clarity is what makes the Survivor stable, but above all else, it's what makes this archetype so adaptable. When the Survivor fails to get a promotion that they worked hard for or struggles with a problem, they aren't concerned with assigning blame or fixating on all the negative ways in which this outcome will impact them. Instead, the Survivor adapts and overcomes or learns something new about themselves or their predicament.

As a human, you have the innate ability to do the same thing, even if this ability is buried under layers of fear, inhibition, and self-doubt. The only reason you're here in the first place is that your ancestors were able to rise above the challenges in their lives. Strength can often come from a sense of purpose and direction in life, so your resilience can gradually develop if you set more goals for yourself. These don't have to start off as major life goals. The important thing is that they pose at least some challenge so that you can practice tackling adversity without pushing the stakes too high.

There is really no way to tap into your innate resilience without facing adversity. You have to actively seek it out and test yourself until you find a level at which you can achieve tangible results. For some people, even getting up early in the morning every day can be a substantial challenge. Life changes that require a bit of effort without being overwhelming can be an excellent start and help you develop a taste for pushing yourself further. These efforts will inevitably provide you with a taste of victory, no matter how small the win might be.

Reconciling with Adversity

Emotional and mental resilience comes naturally to some people, but they can still be developed through concentrated effort. To harness the Survivor within, you have to make an effort to change the way you think about certain situations, especially adversity and setbacks. The first step is to accept that these circumstances are normal parts of life and are virtually unavoidable. Some people can certainly be dealt an unusually difficult hand in life, but on various levels, everyone has to deal with a rough patch every now and then and overcome obstacles. Professional setbacks, family issues, emotional problems, disappointments, and other hurdles will be experienced by everyone at some point.

One way to change the way you deal with these problems is to perceive each failure or challenge as an opportunity to learn, grow, and strengthen yourself. Nature has a way of strengthening living creatures through struggle. Consider the effort and discomfort that it usually takes to build a stronger body through exercise or learn a new skill through studying and practice. These trials are all integral parts of personal progress.

Through some self-training, you can teach yourself to think in the same way about other difficulties, particularly those that you didn't ask for. The key difference is choice because you can choose to go to the gym, but you often can't choose whether or not you're going to experience a rough patch in your life. However, you still get to choose the way in which you approach these problems. With the right mindset, you can reframe almost any setback into a growth opportunity, whether in business, relationships, or any other area of your life. That growth can come from the lessons you glean from your failures or the creative ways in which you adapt to challenging situations.

To resist despair and discouragement and analyze your situations in that way requires a clear mind, which is a skill in and of itself. You can use various methods to try and remain steadfast in difficult times, some long-term and others more immediate. Managing your stress levels through activities like physical exercise, meditation, yoga, or therapy is a sound long-term strategy to alleviate tension and reduce the chances of you cracking under pressure. For more immediate remedies, you can look to mental exercises like mindfulness.

Connecting with yourself through exercise, meditation, or nature can help you become centered.'

Even the simplest mindfulness routine can be a powerful asset to help you remain calm and present in any situation. Mindfulness is all about focusing on a specific thing other than the stressors and distractions around you. A common approach is something called mindful breathing, which entails focusing on your breathing and making it an object of rudimentary meditation. You can do this on the fly because all it requires is that you become mindful and aware of your breathing.

It's not a breathing exercise in the sense that you have to breathe a certain way or to a particular depth. Mindful breathing is all about observing your breathing and maintaining an awareness of it. This can be more complicated than it sounds, especially in stressful situations, but if you analyze your breathing and break it down into a few key elements, it becomes easier to focus on it. Try to equate your breathing with its pattern or the physical sensation of air traveling through your respiratory system.

Practice this at home or when you're running simple chores, and eventually, you'll develop a focus switch that you can turn on at will. With enough practice, you'll find that being mindful of your breathing can almost completely drown out all background noise and empty your mind. This way, you could focus on problem-solving instead of stressing over setbacks. As a result, you'll find it more difficult to distract yourself and find yourself more present.

To harness the Survivor within in a healthy way, you must remember to avoid falling into its shadow side. Above all, this means embracing vulnerability and letting go of your fears. When you interpret it the right way and combine it with common sense and self-care, vulnerability can become a source of power. Allowing yourself to be vulnerable without fear opens you up to relationships, teamwork, public speaking, new experiences, new professional pursuits, and so much more. Unlocking all of these characteristics can hardly be seen as anything but power.

Chapter 4: The Hero – Seeker of Quests and Challenges

Based on Jung's own hero archetype, the Hero of this book also has a few things in common with the Survivor, particularly perseverance. Apart from the ability to persevere through challenges, heroes also tend to be ambitious and are known for their boldness and courage. The Hero is the type who actively seeks out a challenge, on top of having the innate ability to deal with adversity. This chapter will explore one of the bravest archetypes and will show you what it takes to relentlessly pursue excellence in all endeavors.

The Hero, seeker of quests and challenges.[10]

Archetype Profile

One of the key differences between the Survivor and the Hero is the latter's notable drive for achievement. The Survivor can take all comers, but that strength doesn't always come in combination with ambition. Strength and ambition are very different things, and there are a whole lot of people out there who can have one without the other. However, ambition often involves boldness, which the Hero has in spades.

It takes a decisive attitude, free of inhibitions, to dive headfirst into challenges in the relentless pursuit of a goal. The Hero's strength also revolves around their ability to easily find and set those goals, as this archetype can rarely be found lacking purpose or direction. Everyone has the ability to identify what's important to them and make it their life goal, but the Hero is innately blessed with an overarching sense of purpose that informs their unstoppable drive.

The Hero's characteristic courage manifests in many ways, and this archetype is one of the most widespread across cultures and traditions. Tales of human heroism almost always involve the pursuit of a goal in the face of overwhelming odds, as well as leadership, drive, and justice. Indeed, the Hero archetype usually produces leaders who can step up to the plate and take charge even in the most difficult situations. People with a strong Hero archetype tend to exhibit an inspiring presence that not only makes others willing to follow but can also awaken their own hidden strengths.

Constantly pursuing new challenges, the Hero often has an inherent desire to push boundaries, especially those in their own abilities. For this archetype, each challenge is an opportunity to shine and prove their abilities to the world. This doesn't come from a lack of confidence or a desire to compensate for personal shortcomings. The Hero simply craves achievement and is in its element when there's a mission to carry out.

It's also not uncommon for the Hero to be protective of others and possess a strong moral compass, assuming that they don't go too far and give in to vanity or ruthless competition. An individual whose Hero archetype is healthy and strong will have a soothing effect on the people around them, projecting confidence as well as understanding and openness. This is what makes the Hero a good leader and a role model for other people.

The fuel of the Hero's drive is ambition, which comes naturally to this archetype. A challenge can put the Hero into high gear, but the ultimate goal that they're pursuing is what motivates them. The Hero's focus on the goal is unyielding, and the sense of achievement that comes when they succeed affects this archetype with a unique intensity. This is why the Hero will often actively seek out a challenge or quest, chasing the gratification and confirmation that comes from completing a journey. The Hero will also have a taste for transformation, enjoying the act of pushing boundaries and breaking new ground, especially in regards to proving their abilities.

Embodying Ambition and Courage

The Hero is the perfect example of courage not being defined by an absence of fear. Any well-balanced individual ruled by this archetype will certainly retain their common sense, their ability to assess risk, and a sense of uncertainty in certain situations. The Hero's courage is manifested in this archetype's ability to face those fears and continue pursuing goals despite uncertainty. The Hero's ambition and drive simply outweigh any fear that's present, even though that fear can certainly be felt.

Resilience plays a major role in this ability, so if you want to embody the ambition and courage of the Hero, you have to first become more resilient. The best way to do this is to harness and develop your inner Survivor, as discussed in the previous chapter. You can also simply set a range of various challenges for yourself, focusing on growth and self-improvement. The most important thing is to engage in some introspection and analyze yourself and your life to identify areas where you could take decisive steps, no matter how small.

There are a few key areas to attend to with that goal in mind, including your relationships, professional life, hobbies, or other things that bring you fulfillment. There are many ways for a person to seize the initiative and become more courageous, but these are the most important fronts to focus on. In all of these pursuits, you can take small or moderate steps to gradually build up your resilience, confidence, and ambition.

Relationships, in the broadest sense, depend a lot on communication. Many problems in that aspect of life tend to emerge from a breakdown in communication or a lack thereof. If you're not expressing yourself openly and clearly, it can be difficult to clarify your needs and boundaries. Sometimes, courage is manifested in the simple act of outspokenness, free of inhibition and fear. People with a strong Hero archetype won't bottle things up and stay silent when they should speak. If an expression is healthy and clear, it will have a tremendously positive effect on your existing relationships and make things a whole lot easier with any new people you might meet.

Things work similarly in the workplace, where you'll have to be outspoken and forthcoming if you want to prove your worth. The fear of failure, responsibility, or judgment is a common cause of people being held back in their professional development. Learning how to accept criticism and take risks will make it easier for you to put your ideas out there and demonstrate your skills in any professional setting. This basic resilience will inevitably strengthen your confidence and allow your ambition to flourish. Even when your ideas aren't accepted or you falter in a task, the chances are good that your initiative, effort, and interest will be noticed. Specific job skills are merely a matter of learning, whereas initiative is a character trait that's highly appreciated in most professional settings.

Each new day provides opportunities to test and challenge yourself by leaving your comfort zone. If you lack courage and ambition, perhaps it's simply a matter of creating an opportunity for yourself to awaken these strengths. The worst thing you can do is surrender to inertia and avoid trying new things. When you leave your comfort zone, you'll eventually discover passions that you never knew you had, and then you'll start feeling driven.

The Shadow of Reckless Arrogance

As one of the more grandiose and impressive archetypes, the Hero has quite an extensive shadow side that must be taken into account. Apart from the obvious pitfalls, such as the warping of courage into recklessness, many of the Hero's weaknesses have to do with ego. If this archetype loses balance, the individual guided by it can become tremendously egotistical and arrogant. Overconfidence is a common side effect of boldness, and since the Hero has plenty of the latter, he or she must adopt certain checks and balances in the interest of self-restraint.

When the Hero loses control, they can rush into challenges without proper planning, take unnecessary risks, enter into needless conflicts, and much more. Overconfidence can easily spiral into delusions of grandeur and suppress your ability to self-assess. Taking on too big of a challenge before you're ready or trying to get too much stuff done in a short amount of time can quickly land you in a world of trouble. Apart from the immediate damage you can cause through major failures, you can also end up disappointed and experience a confidence crash. Everyone respects a decisive charger, but if you fly too close to the sun, you'll inevitably meet your match and have a hard landing.

The Hero can also burn out mentally and emotionally if they don't set some common-sense limits for themselves. Everyone has a breaking point, and as much as the Hero might love a challenge, they will never be invulnerable. This archetype will benefit immensely from balancing their ambition with self-care and a healthy degree of humility. The latter is a crucial introspective exercise, which requires honest self-analysis and an understanding of your weaknesses. Most importantly, you must understand that it's sometimes essential to seek the support of others and realize that there's no shame in asking for help.

The balance that the Hero needs can be summarized in introspection. This can be difficult for the Hero because this archetype is often very outgoing, goal-oriented, and obsessed with their worldly pursuits. To slow things down and have some time to reflect, the Hero would do well to adopt various self-care rituals and occasionally take some time off. They also need to have honest conversations with the people they trust, asking for feedback and guidance.

Family and trusted friends will tell you when you need to slow down, and their insights can be instrumental in helping you see your limits with clarity. In general, the Hero must remember that soul-searching and self-discovery are quests that should always remain high on their list of challenges to pursue. In fact, the Hero might find that reconciling with their human weaknesses and becoming more modest is *the* challenge of their lifetime.

Since this archetype often has a moral dimension manifested in their strong sense of justice, the Hero can also succumb to self-righteousness. Loving justice and fighting for it is commendable, but you must remember that your sense of justice comes from within you and can be quite subjective. You must allot some time and patience to hear the perspectives and opinions of others, lest you become blinded by your personal sense of justice and morality. Justice shouldn't become just another quest to pursue for personal gratification or self-glorification. It's a universal human ideal in which all people should strive to play a part – *together.*

This archetype has a strong sense of justice.[11]

The Power of Determination

The Hero's strengths are perhaps best summarized in determination, as all of the other qualities in this archetype tend to fit into that one all-encompassing characteristic. The Hero's unwavering focus on goals, headstrong attitude, courage in the face of hardship, ambition, and unending motivation all come together to create determination that's akin to a superpower.

Harnessing the Hero within you can require extensive attitude adjustments, depending on your habits, mentality, and other traits. With the right strategy, however, anyone can awaken their innate natural heroism and use it to their advantage. If you've got a long way to go until you feel that you might be on the path toward heroism, your best course is to be realistic and methodical. If it's not already present, courage must be built up over time, so it's best to have an incremental approach that produces small yet noticeable results on a regular basis.

No matter how small, every victory will contribute to your growing confidence. That's why taking small steps is important instead of setting massive, unrealistic goals that are more likely to lead to short-term failures and long-term disappointment. Every goal you set must toe the fine line of balance between ambition and feasibility. As a start, it's a good idea to experiment with challenges in pursuits that don't affect things like work and other essential areas of your life because this will allow for more creativity and room to maneuver. Make a list of all the ways you could improve yourself, including physical fitness or learning new skills. Analyze these goals, pick the one that feels the most achievable at the time, and develop your plan.

You should meticulously track your progress to harness the full sense of empowerment that your successes will provide. Take a written note of every important milestone or breakthrough in your personal journal, and take some time to reflect on how it makes you feel and what benefits you're observing. The more results you can describe, no matter how small they might seem, the more you'll feel accomplished.

To strengthen your determination and ensure that you stay the course, celebrating each success is a crucial piece of the puzzle. Celebrating your wins should involve some form of reward appropriate for the challenge you're going through. What matters is that it contributes to your sense of accomplishment and allows you to relish in the gratifying feeling of having faced your fears and persevered through hardship.

It's all about positive reinforcement. You want to make the encouraging emotional impact of achievement as tangible as possible so that it's etched in your memory. This way, when you press on with determination, good things will happen. Overcoming your fears is a reward in itself, though, and you'll quickly find that your brain has a deep-seated natural mechanism to reward you for persevering through adversity. The essential strength of the Hero archetype is that they don't have to force themselves through this process to get to the reward. It's the Hero's nature to feel this drive, and the challenge itself is its own reward, but everyone can get to this level with enough dedication and a powerful determination to change.

Becoming Your Story's Hero

It can be somewhat challenging to awaken and harness the Hero archetype within you if it's not already pronounced, but as you can see, it's certainly doable. One way to do this is to develop a taste for achievement, as described above. Remember that your goals don't have to be major life shifts or historic successes, but they should present some tangible challenge that will test you on some level. Once you're able to reach simplistic goals, you can escalate the challenge and gradually work your way up.

It's a good idea to outline what you might call your own "Hero's Journey," which will focus on the past and future, revolving around action as well as analysis. You can create an escalating ladder of challenges that stretches some distance into the future, starting with small courageous steps at the bottom and ending with your major, overarching goals that require years of work. Using your journal, you should go into detail on each of your challenges, especially those that are behind you.

Apart from your recent accomplishments, you should also focus on challenges that you've faced in the more distant past. This includes challenges that ended in failure or ones that you remember for the fear they made you feel, preventing you from even trying. Elaborate on these moments of failure and analyze them for any lessons they might have taught you, trying to apply this knowledge to what lies ahead. Try to identify the exact moments or triggers that made you run away or held you back from success. Analyze where these triggers come from, what made them so discouraging, and how they might show up again when you dive into new challenges.

The more you write about these things, the more material you'll have to analyze. This will help you understand your deeper issues and give you some reference points for future comparisons. After you succeed and prove your courage, you'll be able to reflect on the earlier parts of your Hero's Journey and get a clear picture of how you've progressed and which obstacles you've overcome. Seeing the distance you've traveled will be yet another reward and truly reinforce the idea that you're taking bold new steps toward a life without fear.

Apart from rewarding yourself and celebrating your breakthroughs, you can also draw inspiration and encouragement from outside sources. Try to find empowering stories from people who've had to overcome their fears and beat the odds through determination, especially those stories that feel relatable to your struggles on a personal level. It's never too late to find new role models in your life and absorb new strength from their inspiring examples.

Chapter 5: The Nurturer – Healer of Souls

While the Hero can often have protective traits, the Nurturer takes this selfless characteristic to a whole new level. Having a lot of common ground with Jung's caregiver, this magnanimous archetype is all about helping other people, whether through selfless action, empathy, compassion, understanding, or any other channel through which the Nurturer touches the lives of others. The Nurturer's compassion is more than a personal interest, acting as the primary source of life fulfillment for this archetype. In this chapter, you'll learn all about the most compassionate archetype and the ways in which you can harness its power to become a source of healing in the lives of the people around you.

The Nurturer is the healer of souls.[12]

Archetype Profile

The Nurturer is a naturally empathetic archetype that places a lot of emphasis on other people and their needs. As a result, this archetype cherishes emotional connection and prioritizes relationships. Whereas an archetype such as the Hero might derive meaning and stimulation from overcoming challenges, the Nurturer is in its element when helping other people, hearing out their problems, and helping them improve their emotional well-being.

This archetype's compassion also has a communal dimension in that the Nurturer thrives in communities and has a strong desire to foster emotional harmony in such groups. The Nurturer is a source of support for everyone around them, not just on the emotional front but also in practical terms. The ways in which the Nurturer might help will depend on their particular skills or the situation at hand, but everyone can always count on this archetype to do everything in their power to assist.

Still, the Nurturer is, above all, an emotional being with a deep understanding of other people. This type of person often takes on the role of an emotional healer who knows their way around the hearts of others and can help them resolve internal turmoil. The Nurturer knows what to say and when to say it, possessing a sensitivity to the expressions and emotions of others that enables the archetype to communicate on a higher level. While this archetype doesn't always imply immense passion or overwhelming emotion, these communication skills and sensitivities enable the Nurturer to maintain powerful relationships.

Their communication skills help them keep strong relationships.[18]

Nurturers are also famously generous and tend to emphasize the happiness of others more than their own benefit. This goes beyond emotional support and often translates into material generosity as well. The Nurturer derives immense joy from charity and is completely in sync with their emotional core when making donations or giving presents. This generosity is directed at friends, family, and strangers alike. The Nurturer in your life is the kind of person who'll come up with a special present for your birthday or the holidays, especially if they know you well.

Relationships are very important for the Nurturer, enhanced by strong emotional connection and selflessness. Even when all else fails in life, this archetype will still try to find ways to maintain relationships and keep them from falling apart. Unfortunately, the Nurturer can sometimes neglect their own emotional needs entirely, which presents its own problems.

In general, the Nurturer is an archetype that everyone would be lucky to have in their life. As the pillar of the community and someone to lean on, the Nurturer enriches life for everyone around them and makes them feel more secure. Whether you need emotional and moral support or someone to stand by your side when the going gets rough, the Nurturer will be there to pick you up if you fall. Playing this role yourself can be challenging and will entail a lot of responsibility, but the emotional fulfillment that comes from it can be immense.

Embodying Compassion

There are two basic components to unlocking and utilizing your Nurturer archetype. These are empathy and non-judgment. While it might seem like these two qualities always come in the same package, this isn't necessarily true. It's possible to empathize with others in the sense that you can understand them and put yourself in their shoes, but that won't always stop you from passing judgment. Likewise, you can be the least judgmental person in the room, but that won't always help you understand other people and their emotions on a deeper level.

Some folks are naturally predisposed to powerful empathetic responses and don't have a judgmental bone in their body, but nurture plays an essential role as well. Non-judgment and empathy can both be developed and strengthened through a few practical changes in the way you interact with people. One of the most powerful tools toward that end is active listening. The art of active listening exists somewhere between sitting emotionlessly like a stone while pretending to listen and interrupting or hijacking someone's monologue. Respectively, these two extremes usually embody apathy and judgment.

Active listening occurs when you express an authentic interest in what the other person is saying, showing genuine empathy and being respectful. The key element is your ability to encourage that person to keep talking and express themselves in more detail. This is done with verbal and non-verbal cues, all of which boil down to simple signals that you are being responsive. Eye contact, nodding, and other physical signs constitute non-verbal cues in active listening.

Verbal cues include things like short, one-word confirmations and simple yet open-ended questions that keep a conversation going. Open-ended questions work so well because they prompt your conversational partner to provide more context and go into detail, helping both of you get to the bottom of the emotions and concerns at play. Usually, short questions can be thrown in at any point in the conversation, but the perfect moment is when the other person finishes a statement.

When these cues are free of judgment, they will have a powerful effect on other people and enrich every conversation they have with you. Active listening comes naturally to the Nurturer archetype, but as you can see, it's a fairly straightforward behavioral adaptation that anyone can use. The best part about active listening is that it will inevitably enhance your empathy as a direct consequence of learning more about people. This might just be the thing that awakens your inner Nurturer.

Beyond communication, you can also try to summon this archetype by making a conscious effort to come up with different ways of being supportive. You'll need to reflect on yourself, the people you care about, and all the other folks you interact with. Try to think about all those moments that might provide opportunities for you to support others, whether through simple acts of kindness or more substantive care. You can think of this as a creative exercise, analyzing other people's needs and trying to tailor your approach to them. The end goal is to make them feel appreciated, understood, and cared for – all of which are effects that the Nurturer naturally has on the people around them.

The Shadow of Self-Neglect

People who fall under the shadow of the Nurturer archetype can be notoriously self-neglecting. This is the point where sacrifice, selflessness, and the service of others become major faults that can cause a plethora of problems in a person's life. Unlike the Pure Soul archetype, the Nurturer doesn't have to be naive in order for this to happen. Other people don't have to scheme and conspire to use the Nurturer's goodwill or try to manipulate them. The people that the Nurturer is helping can be the kindest and most trusted friends or family members, yet if the Nurturer forgets their own needs, they can fall into ruin.

The Nurturer can also overextend to the point where their abilities simply falter. This archetype's belief that they can and should help everyone in the world can develop into a savior complex, featuring overprotectiveness, too much intrusion into other people's lives, and complete burnout. If the Nurturer overestimates their own abilities and becomes obsessive, they might take on so many burdens at once that they simultaneously fail everyone.

It's better to give a single person the attention that they deserve and help them instead of trying to help ten people at once and getting nothing done. Not only will this lead to negative outcomes in a practical sense, but the Nurturer can collapse into profound disappointment and feelings of inadequacy. This archetype's inclination to help is an unconscious need more than a preference, so their potential inability to help can easily become a debilitating fear.

To avoid this pitfall and prevent yourself from becoming dangerously codependent, you must learn to recognize your symptoms of emotional exhaustion. A common sign is when you never spare a moment's thought for your own problems, remaining perpetually focused on others. You might succumb to an overwhelming feeling that you're responsible for everything and everyone. The feelings of other people might become overbearing and affect you in an unhealthy manner. It's also common for suffering Nurturers to be overly self-critical, feel guilty or ashamed, or experience daily fatigue. You might experience a range of other, more personal signs, so it's essential that you reflect on how you're feeling and occasionally talk about it.

This is why Nurturers must establish boundaries. You can do this by learning to say no to people or simply by conducting an honest, objective assessment of your abilities. Understanding your limits can be absolutely decisive in helping any Nurturer live a more balanced life. This process also involves the acceptance of some harsh realities about the world as a whole. You must understand that you're a single individual in an enormous world that's ridden with problems.

You cannot always help everyone, and some people might not even want your help, even if you're convinced that they need it. Start by doing what you can to help yourself and help those who are close to you before you expand your focus to larger problems. You must also be aware that it's difficult to be in a relationship with someone who doesn't love themselves. If you neglect yourself and let your mental and emotional health decline, you'll inevitably become difficult to live with. The people who love you will want to support and help you just as you do for them, but they'll find that difficult if you never allow yourself any self-care.

The Pillar of Support and Forgiveness

This archetype's nurturing nature can have a profound effect on the lives they touch and the communities they belong to. The Nurturer's transformative influence can put out fires, resolve conflicts, mend bridges, and guide people on a path toward happiness. If you're a born Nurturer, you would be justified in considering this role to be a superpower. It's about much more than carrying someone's groceries or giving them a piece of friendly advice. The Nurturer's presence is strongly felt by other people, and its effects can be nothing short of life-changing.

However, the tremendous impact of their role doesn't make the Nurturer egotistical or arrogant, which would be completely contrary to their kind nature. The Nurturer truly sees other people first, and they simply don't put personal interest into the equation. When they analyze other people's problems, the main objective is always to bring that person closer to a state of emotional harmony and wellness. They also don't require gratitude, even though they should. The inner feeling of having helped someone is the Nurturer's ultimate reward.

Because they are humble and selfless, Nurturers won't cling to grudges because they'll rarely interpret other people's transgressions as personal or irredeemable. A well-rounded Nurturer will certainly learn lessons and not permit being fooled or abused, but they won't hold ill will or harbor resentment on an emotional level. This leaves them open to forgiveness and renewed cooperation if issues with another person can be ironed out in a rational manner that benefits everyone.

This capacity for reconciliation and forgiveness makes the Nurturer a highly constructive partner in all human endeavors. There are no personal feelings born of injured egos that will stand in the way when it comes to Nurturers. Overall, it's difficult to truly burn a bridge with such people, as they'll always leave at least some room for redemption. This opens the Nurturer up to civilized communication, not repeated abuse, assuming that they know how to set boundaries and look after themselves.

Balancing Caregiving

Stimulating your Nurturer archetype on a basic level is rather simple. All you have to do is tap into your natural empathy and engage in acts of kindness. You'll naturally develop a taste for it after a while, and you can eventually progress from basic compassion to having a tremendous positive influence on other people's lives. In accordance with your living situation and routine, try to identify three small daily acts of kindness that you can do to have an effect on others.

Make a personalized checklist that works for you, and make sure that you stick with it. These can be minor acts like compliments or making a fresh pot of coffee for your coworkers. If you're not used to this, you might be surprised by how receptive and touched most people will be if you make the slightest kind gesture. After you get the hang of it, you can continue building yourself into a Nurturer through more concrete steps. However, you must always remember this archetype's shadow and make sure that you're becoming a Nurturer, not a fool.

Keeping the Nurturer within you healthy entails some reflection and emotional self-care. As usual, one of the best ways to engage in such introspection is to keep a journal of your thoughts and feelings. Prompt yourself to make at least a weekly entry summarizing all the ways in which you've recently helped someone, whether physically or emotionally. Describe the situations while also writing down how each of those instances made you feel and why. While it might seem counterintuitive, this can help your self-care.

Once you have a somewhat extensive written record of your caregiving moments toward other people, you can use it in two main ways. Firstly, you should try to determine which of the things that you've done for other people are those that you'd like to see reciprocated more often. At least for a moment, try to disregard the fulfillment that you naturally get from being helpful. Through an objective lens, figure out the reciprocities that could be beneficial to you. If any such reciprocity exists, then you'll know that the people in your life are appreciative and willing to give back.

On the other hand, if you end up only with a list of things that you've done for others without any acknowledgment or goodwill from the other side, then you should consider setting up some boundaries. This is the second way in which you'll use your journal entries. If you find that any of your helpful moments required immense effort or self-sacrifice on your part, and yet you've received no kindness in return, then perhaps you should tone things down in the future.

The Nurturer derives pleasure from helping others, but this fulfillment can be achieved in less sacrificial ways. This is the essence of the Nurturer's self-care, and it boils down to objective self-analysis and balance. The benefit of maintaining a written record of your Nurturer journey is that it facilitates impartial analysis. The Nurturer is often helpful on impulse and even foregoes logic when their instincts kick in after seeing a person in need. What's more, the Nurturer will quickly forget about the help he provided after the fact because it's not in this archetype's nature to consider their helpfulness a favor and take mental notes of the things they do for others. A journal will offset such fallacies, ground you in reality, and allow the kind of rational analysis that's only possible in retrospect.

Beyond introspection and making sure that you're not taken advantage of, you should also engage in other forms of self-care. You can create what you might call a self-care toolkit, which consists of personalized strategies and activities that are meant to recharge your batteries. At least once a week, you should devote some time to such activities to give yourself an emotional and physical break. Whatever it is that you enjoy, you should formulate a routine around it and be kind to yourself.

Chapter 6: The Explorer – Pursuer of New Horizons

Embodying the traits of archetypes such as the seeker or wanderer, the Explorer is an amalgam of human traits that are all about exploration, discovery, growth, and liberty. This archetype refuses to be boxed in and will always find a way to break free and pursue new horizons. The Explorer's overwhelming curiosity routinely overshadows any fear of the unknown and enables this archetype to embark on epic journeys, both in the real world and in their own soul. This chapter will investigate the most adventurous archetype and show you how to use it to bring some excitement into your life while keeping its restless nature under some control.

The Explorer is the pursuer of new horizons.[14]

Archetype Profile

The defining characteristics of the Explorer are curiosity and independence. These two factors drive most of the other things that this archetype does, fueling their restless nature and unquenchable thirst for new experiences. If there's one thing the Explorer can't abide by, it's being stuck in place – especially as a consequence of external forces. They have an unwavering, deep-seated desire to experience life to its fullest before they die, and they'll pursue that fulfillment on all fronts.

For the Explorer, adventure will often entail physical movement, but it's much more than that. This archetype will find and pursue adventures through travel, learning, soul-searching, and much more. There are few things in life that the Explorer values more than personal freedom. A lot of this adventure-seeking is about personal growth, which the Explorer perceives as inseparably intertwined with experience and discovery.

The discovery that the Explorer chases has external and internal dimensions. This archetype can be pronounced in people who have vastly different characters and interests, which will determine the way in which they seek adventure. An outwardly oriented Explorer will get their kicks from traveling and exploring new cultures and locations. On the other hand, an Explorer can also be rather introverted, focused on their internal struggles, spirituality, and intellectual pursuits. One Explorer's adventurousness can revolve around sights and sounds, while another's can be all about learning and finding new ways of thinking. Of course, some Explorers might also be interested in all of the above.

The important thing for the Explorer is to keep moving and feel confident that they are unrestricted. When individuals with this archetype are forced to stay in place, they will quickly start to feel trapped, regardless of whether they're standing still mentally or physically. Luckily, Explorers can often be highly creative in what they consider to be an adventure. Depending on their personal interests and preferences, Explorers can find adventure in things that other people don't find stimulating or even interesting. As you can imagine, the Explorer archetype can do wonders if it works in unison with the Pure Soul archetype. When combined, the former's hunger for adventure and the latter's excited mind that's easy to impress can find fulfillment with ease.

Venturing into the unknown is the common denominator that motivates both inner and outer journeys for the Explorer. An individual guided by this archetype can be an adrenaline junky, a seasoned traveler, or a bookworm. While these lifestyles are vastly different at face value, the Explorer archetype doesn't really care what channel it uses to get its exploratory fulfillment. As such, it's a highly accommodating archetype from which people from all walks of life can benefit. There is an innate inclination toward exploration that most human beings naturally share, to some extent, which makes this archetype very universal and desirable.

Embodying Adventure and Discovery

The Explorer archetype describes a person who refuses to be caged in or held back by any external constraints. They might impose limits on themselves if they're trying to lead a balanced life, but they'll often find reasons to tread beyond their comfort zone and penetrate personal limits as well. The Explorer isn't unhinged or reckless if the archetype is in balance. On the contrary, the Explorer can be highly organized, careful, and reasonable, but their drive comes from their adventurous spirit.

Embodying this archetype means embracing discovery and pursuing new experiences with openness. People can get into adventures and go on great journeys while still being closed off and inhibited. They can be fearful of change and transformation and avoid gaining deeper insights if they feel that such discoveries can upset their life. Explorers don't have this problem, allowing themselves to open up and fully embrace all that is new or unknown.

A large part of the Explorer's quest in life revolves around personal identity. This is why their craving for discovery has such a strong internal dimension as well. The Explorer is often struck by questions of who they are, where they belong, where they're going, and what their purpose is. Some of them might dive deeply into existentialism, spirituality, and meditation, but this doesn't make them vulnerable to existential dread or doubt. Rather, the Explorer is excited by each prospect for discovery and learning, whether it's about their own self or the world as a whole.

Cultivating your own adventurous spirit is one of those things that are simple to say yet complex under the surface. On a basic level, all you have to do to embody the Explorer archetype is take a decisive step outside your comfort zone. This is something you can do in your daily life through a million baby steps. Examples include saying the things you normally wouldn't, taking a road you usually don't, calling up an old friend, or trying a new, uncharacteristic outfit. It doesn't matter what it is, in a physical sense, as long as it involves a degree of change and shakes things up.

Leaving your comfort zone is about much more than physical activity, though. There is also an intellectual dimension in which you'll leave comfort by exploring new perspectives, hearing unusual or disagreeable opinions, reading different literature, and other such thought-provoking actions. To leave your comfort zone, you simply have to risk being uncomfortable to refresh your life and broaden your horizons. The Explorer embodies this lifestyle by natural impulse because the archetype is driven by the very feeling of discomfort that's inherent to the unknown. Since the Explorer doesn't fear it, that discomfort becomes something that's welcomed and actively sought out.

It can be a tricky concept to wrap your head around, initially, but it's an acquired taste for people whose Explorer archetype isn't naturally pronounced. Once you dive headfirst into the unknown, your instincts will kick in, and you'll understand how growth and discovery can only occur beyond the walls of your comfort zone. New hobbies, places, people, leisurely activities, and knowledge will all help you foster a sense of adventure and progression.

The Shadow of Avoidance and Restlessness

As an archetype that craves adventure, the Explorer is naturally restless. This restlessness is merely the fuel of the Explorer's drive if it's kept in check and harnessed constructively. However, it has its negative implications as well. Literally and figuratively, some Explorers can find it challenging to just sit still and feel the moment. This can diminish the value of the Explorer's journeys and affect their relationships, which are essential to human happiness regardless of the dominant archetype.

The shadow Explorer's harm to relationships comes primarily from an inability to commit. When they lose control, Explorers might constantly crave something new to the point where even a loving, functional relationship starts to feel like a trap. This is why you mustn't pursue new experiences just for experience's sake or for shallow kicks. A balanced Explorer chases the unknown because of the things that can be learned there, not because they need a way to escape their daily life or compensate for some kind of emotional emptiness.

When novelty itself becomes an obsession, the Explorer's pursuits will lose depth. New experiences need to be properly integrated through introspection, analysis, and learning, not just stacked up for simplistic excitant. The fulfillment that comes from shallow novelty is short-term and will only leave you craving more as it gradually starts to resemble an addiction. If there are problem areas in your life, they need to be addressed and improved, not buried under mounds of excitement and restless trailblazing.

After a period of exploration and discovery, you should follow up with some downtime and reflection before chasing the next thing. Keep a journal or focus on something else that has to do with your regular life. You need to develop an ability to remain comfortable even when nothing special is going on. Otherwise, the Explorer will never be satisfied. In other words, you need to find ways to ground yourself and focus on your long-term fulfillment. There must be something consistent in your life that acts as a thread to connect all of your experiences and gives life its continuity. You can call this your "constant," and it can be a fulfilling job, a creative hobby, a sport, or a loving relationship.

The Explorer needs to balance life by taking time out to rest.[14]

If the Explorer is able to overcome its shadow and achieve balance while also having some luck in finding meaningful relationships that provide just enough grounding and guidance, then this archetype can be the recipe for the most fulfilling life imaginable. That's even truer if they can find a kindred spirit that also draws its strength from the Explorer archetype. When two Explorers team up and truly understand each other, their common journey can lead to positively profound discoveries.

It's also worth pointing out that bad relationships can feel like a trap regardless of the archetypes involved. Sometimes, you might be right to feel trapped, and this may have nothing to do with your natural desire for freedom. It's important to be analytical and honest so that you can differentiate between a toxic relationship and simple restlessness on your part. The Explorer isn't always to blame when their relationships fall apart.

Freedom Incarnate

The Explorer's love for freedom and exploration isn't some spoiled child's impulse. This archetype lives and breathes their liberty and knows how to run after it with determination. As such, the Explorer is truly independent and self-sufficient. This profound independence is perhaps the Explorer's greatest superpower, as this archetype can create and absorb fulfillment entirely on its own. These individuals are their own source of motivation and drive, needing very little external encouragement or guidance.

To be so fundamentally independent is to divorce one's sense of happiness and life fulfillment from the influence of other people. This liberates the Explorer in a way that few other archetypes can realize. This is also why Explorers often find it difficult to settle down and ground themselves in reality, which can be a problem in many spheres of life, not just relationships. Still, most Explorers are more than willing to pay the price and sacrifice other aspects of living in the interest of their freedom to pursue their adventures. As long as those sacrifices are affordable and reasonable, the Explorer can successfully leverage their independence for a fully liberated life without much damage on other fronts.

To harness the strength of your Explorer archetype, you should try and see life as a continuous journey of growth and learning. You must subordinate novelty, adventure, and the overall chase for growth and learning so that the learning journey is the ultimate motivation. When you start thinking that way, you'll find it easier to see value in new experiences, but you'll also ensure that your explorations have depth and provide you with long-term benefits.

Your inner Explorer should be fed through curiosity, which you sometimes have to actively cultivate. Think of your curiosity as a small flame in your mind that you have to maintain by feeding it fuel. When that fire is extinguished, you have to build it up again, which is best done through practical exploration goals. If you're lucky, your curiosity might return on its own, but your best bet is a proactive approach where you'll seek out new points of interest in the outside world and in your mind.

Take small steps, even if it feels forced, and start exploring your close surroundings both physically and mentally. With enough effort, you will inevitably encounter something new that piques your interest and rekindles the flame. Keep your journal handy whether you're traveling or just exploring your hometown. Set clearly defined exploration goals with an escalating complexity, and make a written note of everything you discover or think, no matter how minuscule.

Awakening Your Taste for Adventure

The Explorer is one of the easier archetypes to invigorate since all you really need to do is expose yourself to new experiences and novelty. If these things are lacking in your life and you feel that you've lost your sense of adventure and exploration, the first thing to do is to create a bucket list of experiences that you find inspiring. This list can include goals that are more difficult to achieve and will require considerable planning, but you should also add a few experiences that are fully feasible in the short term.

When people lose their appetite for adventure, there are often engaging activities that they can take up, which they simply don't get around to because of inertia, a lack of motivation, or a busy schedule. This is where your bucket list should begin. Give yourself a quick rundown of your interests and try to come up with new ways of stimulating those interests. Don't worry about whether these interests and activities are objectively fascinating or what other people might think. Awakening your inner Explorer is all about you, and you'll want to strengthen your sense of independence while you're at it.

Travel is the most obvious form of adventure that many people default to when they want to make their lives more exciting. Immersing yourself in new cultures can be an eye-opening experience with important implications for your character development. Travel allows you to pursue new horizons in a literal sense, but it will do the same on the intellectual, spiritual, and emotional planes. A great way to invigorate your adventurous side while also fostering independence is to travel by yourself, as long as you exercise caution and common sense.

Becoming more adventurous also depends on your ability to derive enjoyment from the things you do by being more present and grounded. As discussed earlier in the book, basic mindfulness can help you immerse yourself and derive more enjoyment from your experiences. You can combine mindfulness with all sorts of activities, especially outdoors. For instance, you might want to create your own mindfulness walks when going to the park or, even better, taking a hike out in nature.

Natural environments will often present plenty of stimuli and things to focus on, so your mindfulness exercises can revolve around things other than your breathing. Birds chirping or the wind rustling the leaves of trees can become your objects of focus and make you more mindful of your surroundings. This is a great way to get out of your own head and embrace the outside world, fostering your outgoing side.

What you choose to do won't matter too much as long as it involves some novelty and leaves room for discovery. Whether you're discovering things about the world around you or about yourself, you can make this feeling stick by keeping a record of the things you find. Consider starting a discovery journal where you can write down all your observations and feelings for subsequent analysis. Preserving the details of your explorations in writing will deepen your appreciation for any journey because there will be a lot of impressions and thoughts that'll occur only in retrospect.

Chapter 7: The Rebel – Challenger of Norms

The Rebel is another archetype that has a lot to do with the love of freedom, although it embodies this pursuit differently from the Explorer. Inspired by the Jungian archetype commonly referred to as the outlaw or revolutionary, the Rebel is all about defiance and change. This archetype is comfortable when challenging rules, conventions, norms, and traditions, particularly in the interest of change, through the questioning of authority. As a fairly disruptive archetype, the Rebel is a complex character with the potential for greatness but also for destruction. However, walking the fine line of balance can make the Rebel one of the most liberating archetypes to cultivate.

The Rebel challenges the norms of society.[16]

Archetype Profile

The Rebel archetype is a chronically nonconforming character who questions everything and generally has a distaste for all things dogmatic or unchanging. It's not that the Rebel will necessarily be disrespectful, as they can certainly observe some rules. However, the Rebel's core instinct is that no rules should be beyond scrutiny. As such, the rules have to make sense if the Rebel is going to respect them. This naturally lands the Rebel in some degree of defiance, most of the time, since virtually anything in life can be scrutinized if the mind is skeptical.

For the Rebel, problems arise when they are asked to obey without question or when others try to forbid them from scrutinizing the norms that they are expected to follow. The Rebel doesn't care for blind obedience or arbitrary conventions that are observed by default simply for the sake of obedience, tradition, or any kind of collective or individual inertia. A truly skeptical Rebel will apply the same principles to their own life, conduct, and beliefs, asking tough questions and second-guessing the motivations behind the things they do and the choices they make.

To constantly challenge authority and ask hard questions, one must be bold and courageous. The Rebel is both of these things, often exhibiting an impressive level of confidence. A lot of Rebels tend to be extroverted, outspoken, and opinionated since their defiance often requires them to openly speak their minds and stand up for what they believe in. Nonetheless, the Rebel can also be the silent type, as resistance can be expressed by quiet yet firm opposition.

The Rebel doesn't seek out adversity for the thrill of the challenge but is more than prepared to face it for the right cause. When this archetype feels that the status quo is undeserving of being upheld, they will feel a powerful drive to uproot it. In pursuit of that goal, the Rebel will make sacrifices and pay a hefty price if the cause demands it. Challenging the status quo and pushing boundaries is how the Rebel thrives, especially when the changes they pursue are clearly defined and in accordance with this individual's morals.

This drive has both a social and personal dimension for the Rebel. Sometimes, they'll challenge external authority to pursue societal changes and transform communities. In other cases, the authority to be challenged is the one in the Rebel's own psyche. The Rebel is rarely completely satisfied with their own state of being and will actively seek out ways to change their behavior, thinking, and character. For this archetype, internal and self-imposed constraints can sometimes feel just as suffocating as those that come from the outside.

Above all, Rebels demonstrate their courage through a willingness to resist despite the consensus. The Rebel doesn't mind traveling a lonely road and will go against the grain no matter the opposition as long as the goal justifies the effort. Popular opinions and majority beliefs have little sway over the course that the Rebel will choose, and they will take on the whole world without allies if they have to. While impressive, this level of determination and courage can also land the Rebel in hot water.

Embodying Defiance

This archetype is in its element when its defiance is kept in check by a strong moral compass. The Rebel must know why they are resisting certain rules instead of just blindly following their natural impulse to resist. The Rebel embodies defiance with courage, but only if they find a worthy cause that leads to a righteous struggle. In the absence of such a cause, the Rebel can become directionless while still maintaining their hardheaded disposition.

To embody and harness this archetype constructively, you must strike a fine balance between defiance and respect. You have to ask questions whenever appropriate, yet you must maintain a level of courtesy and respect in how you approach other people. This becomes easier when you have a set of clearly defined scruples and a high level of moral integrity. Defiance shouldn't be a basic instinct or impulse but a choice, or rather a series of choices that you consciously make. If you make the right choices, your Rebel archetype will become a force for good.

Because of its association with Jung's outlaw archetype, the Rebel is often misunderstood. The outlaw archetype itself is also not inherently destructive despite the word's deceptively negative connotation. In this context, the word "outlaw" should be taken at face value as it simply describes a person who is comfortable operating beyond the bounds of established rules. While this person is inherently disruptive, it's easy to imagine many situations where disrupting the established order is not just appropriate but morally necessary. As such, any outlaw or Rebel can have a negative or positive arc of development, depending entirely on their choices.

Making the right moral choices will put the Rebel on the path of becoming a visionary, revolutionary, protector, activist, or even a great artist. On the flip side of that coin, the Rebel who foregoes moral integrity and humane principles can end up becoming a criminal or an extremist. Overall, all Rebels possess the same instincts of defiance, but it is their moral constitution that will ensure that these instincts are used constructively and as a force for good.

If you want to encourage and harness your inner Rebel in daily life, you can start by developing a habit of questioning the things around you while making sure you hold onto the basics of courteous behavior. In your personal life and professional pursuits, you'll have many opportunities to question norms and challenge the established conventions that oppress you. Your most powerful tool for rational rebellion will be the art of critical thinking, which is a skill to be learned and maintained.

Thinking about things critically will ensure that you ask questions where appropriate, dissect things logically, and always understand your motivations and reasons for asking. Critical thinking will separate your balanced rebelliousness from that of a disruptor who acts solely on impulse. The first step is to make sure that your concerns are objective and based on an impartial analysis of the situation instead of on emotions. For example, suppose you are questioning an established methodology at your workplace. In that case, you want to make sure that you're doing so because you have identified ways in which these things can be changed for the better, not because you dislike your boss and want to stir up the pot.

A rational approach will make it clear to everyone that you're acting in good faith, have integrity, and are respectful. When your criticisms of the rules are well-reasoned and thought-out, people will take your concerns much more seriously and be more accommodating. The embodiment of a wise Rebel is in the ability to carefully consider all the variables and gradually steer things toward change while causing minimal upset for other people.

However, if you pursue change and disrupt the system for long enough, you'll inevitably encounter pushback, no matter how reasonable you are. If your logic is sound, you will be able to recognize when all other options have been exhausted and entering into battle becomes necessary. In those moments, your time for righteous struggle will come, and the way you carried yourself up to that point might decide if you'll have allies at your side.

The Shadow of the Causeless Rebel

If it envelops the Rebel, the shadow side will likely turn this archetype into the stereotypical rebel without a cause or a lonesome crusader on a fruitless journey to nowhere. An unwise, inconsiderate Rebel will become impulsive, reckless, or completely alienated, which can ruin their life and the lives of those around them. As defiant hard chargers, most Rebels have a degree of impulsivity and recklessness within them, but these traits have a way of alternating between flaw and virtue depending on individual character.

Apart from critical thinking, as discussed above, the Rebel would also be wise to practice mindfulness and active listening – and remain open to feedback and different perspectives. The Rebel can become consumed by their own crusade to the point where they develop intellectual tunnel vision and become immune to good advice or valid criticism. This is a bad place to be for anyone, but the Rebel's drive and hardheadedness can make this archetype particularly destructive. When the Rebel gets it into their head that a certain system should be brought down and becomes closed off to constructive feedback, they can pursue their disruptive goal to the bitter end.

History is filled with examples of righteous revolutions, but it also has plenty of stories about calamities resulting from the best of intentions. In regular life, relationships, and professional endeavors, it's often best to err on the side of reform rather than full-blown revolution. That means gradual changes through critical analyses and an assertive attitude in expressing your opinions clearly. There are certain situations in life when radical and sudden changes are needed, such as cutting ties with a toxic person or beating an addiction. Most of the time, however, daily concerns and pressures can be resolved with more restraint.

Thoughtful consideration is the ultimate antidote to the Rebel's inherent impulsivity, and it's the best way to ensure that your actions lead to constructive changes instead of chaos. Your judgment has to be clean and reasonable so that you're able to identify those situations when radical action is the only option left. You don't want to succumb to a reactive mindset that leads you straight into action without a moment's thought.

The best way to prevent this type of error is to work on your mindfulness and restraint by taking a short pause before responding to situations. Whenever you feel that you're being oppressed and unjustly constrained, you must remind yourself not to lash out immediately. Try to focus on your breathing or develop a mantra that keeps you focused and collected. You'll find that delaying your response even by less than a minute will give you ample room to consider a situation from multiple angles and plot out the best course through rational thinking rather than your impulse to rebel.

The Power of Defiance

The Rebel's strength is in this archetype's inclination to question everything and stand firm in their beliefs. This gives them a natural layer of shielding that makes them difficult to manipulate and abuse. The Rebel is an obstacle to overbearing traditions and established structures that keep people in check. Some Rebels will go down as historical figures by externalizing this nature on a global scale, but everyday life is also full of more discrete Rebels who actively challenge the norms and constraints of their small personal worlds.

Defiance is strong in the Rebel.[17]

They are in local communities, offices, and any rules-based groups of people you can imagine. These everyday Rebels carry out thousands of minor daily rebellions that go unnoticed by the world as a whole, yet the combined effect of these individual acts of defiance will gradually drive change on a much wider scale. Some revolutions occur only in the mind, but that doesn't make them any less important.

Whenever an individual, anywhere in the world, questions and rejects an unjust authority or undergoes a positive intellectual transformation, a small victory is won for humanity. As such, the Rebel archetype is an essential element of human conduct and development, and it's one of the key factors that allow societies to progress and improve. That's why the Rebel's relentlessly defiant nature can aptly be characterized as a human superpower.

Apart from courageous defiance, Rebels often possess other powerful traits, such as creativity and leadership. Their leadership role becomes prominent in times of strife and transformation, as this is when they truly come into their own, utilizing their ability to visualize change and direct the uprising toward a constructive goal. The Rebel can be a lone wolf, but they're also often found organizing groups of people and engaging in activism.

Harnessing Constructive Defiance

There are many ways to encourage the emergence of your Rebel archetype and put it to good use. The first step is always to take a close look at your life and identify those areas where you feel constrained, pressured, or otherwise tied down. These can be certain repeating situations, your job, a specific project at your job, or a person and your relationship with them. Only you will know which aspect of your life makes you feel like you want to break out and liberate yourself.

Each of those situations can present a unique set of circumstances that require specific actions on your part if you are to challenge them and create changes. As such, it's a good idea to develop a specific plan on how you're going to rebel against these things. In relationships, this can mean putting your foot down and opening up some difficult topics of conversation. At work, you might have to stand up for your or someone else's rights or demand that your efforts are appreciated and rewarded more.

Whatever the specifics are, you should consider all the variables and devise an approach that strikes a fine balance between reward and blowback. The art of fruitful and positive systemic disruption is in causing the least amount of damage and chaos for maximum gain. This requires finesse and thoughtfulness in how you approach conflict, which will largely depend on your ability to present solid arguments and poke holes in the established order through rational, valid criticism. It's also worth noting that successfully upending the order doesn't have to result in your total victory. Sometimes, a good compromise can be enough of a victory.

If you want to allow your inner Rebel to truly run free, it's a good idea to find causes that align with your values and make you passionate. You can then engage in social activism through volunteer organizations or activist groups and leave your mark. This can profoundly stoke the flames of your inherent rebelliousness because you might get to see your efforts lead to observable changes in the real world.

You don't have to move mountains overnight, but having your voice be heard in the pursuit of a meaningful cause can be empowering and motivate you to get involved on a whole new level. You can start small by writing a list of ideas and causes that you want to advocate for and then look up communities and groups that will allow you to get active at the local level.

When chasing a cause, it's important not to neglect personal growth. If you disregard your inner battles and leave your internal constraints unaddressed, activism might become a way for you to compensate for personal shortcomings. Worse yet, it can provide you with a distraction and an excuse to avoid committing to personal growth. If you don't rebel against your internal factors of self-oppression, which most people have on some level, you'll have difficulty in helping others as compared to if you were truly liberated.

Chapter 8: The Heartkeeper – Lover of Emotions

If the Nurturer archetype had a cousin, it would certainly be the Heartkeeper. However, this archetype shares many characteristics with Jung's lover archetype, which embodies love and passion in the broadest sense. Of all the archetypes that possess emotional depth, the Heartkeeper is perhaps the most relentlessly emotional. It's an archetype that has the nurturing traits and the desire for harmony of the Nurturer - but is embellished by an overwhelming, unrivaled passion. This chapter will focus on this sensitive archetype and explore how it relates to profound human feelings and relationships.

The Heartkeeper is a lover of emotions.[18]

Archetype Profile

When it's said that the Heartkeeper is all about love, there is a lot more in the equation than just romantic inclinations, and the same applies to passion. The Heartkeeper is the embodiment of intense emotion, empathy, and nurturing in all interactions and endeavors. This is the kind of individual who makes decisions and does everything based on love, and whatever they do is driven by relentless passion.

Romantic connections in the Heartkeeper's life are intense, but this archetype applies that same love to friendships, familial relationships, and wider communities. Their heartfelt actions and gestures toward others are often inspiring for the people around them, allowing this archetype to cultivate goodness in other people through the power of their love and its example. Deep emotional connections are what the Heartkeeper seeks and craves with other people and various other aspects of life. Heartkeepers are at their best when they feel as if they are one with their loved ones, their work, and their environment on an emotional level.

This archetype is incredibly intimate and devoted, and it also carries a high degree of sincerity and openness. That sincerity is especially manifested in the clarity and intensity with which the Heartkeeper displays emotions. That's not to say that the Heartkeeper has no filter or has a tendency to fly off the handle. On the contrary, the Heartkeeper will often default to love, and that's the emotion they prefer to express. The power of their emotions depends on how real and heartfelt they are and how plainly obvious that is to everyone. Like any archetype, the Heartkeeper has a shadow side, but their healthy state is one of positivity, devotion, and nurturing.

In work and other human endeavors, love will be either a weakness or strength for the Heartkeeper. Because it's so important for them to feel love in everything they do, Heartkeepers will struggle if their work doesn't evoke such passion. Even if the work is objectively meaningful, consequential, or gainful, the Heartkeeper will still feel weakened if they don't truly enjoy what they're doing. This is why Heartkeepers need to find their way and settle into a profession that agrees with their emotional disposition and the objects of their passion. Still, the Heartkeeper is passionate by nature. With the right approach, these individuals can still find things to be passionate about in most circumstances, thanks to their emotional charge. They can draw on these emotions to inspire action, change their perspective, and transfer energy into those areas of life that need it.

The Heartkeeper has the power to lead by example as well, and they don't have to be assertive to do so. The actions and gestures of this archetype can be so sincere that they have a disarming effect on other people, leading them to join in with their own kindness and desire to reciprocate. It's a fundamental method of communication that exists on a profoundly emotional level, channeled primarily through empathy. The Heartkeeper can be so overwhelmingly devoted and loving that it's impossible for people to stay indifferent.

Embodying Passion

Passion is the overarching force that's shared among all Heartkeepers. It's the ultimate driver that keeps the Heartkeeper going and is one of the defining characteristics of this archetype. There are many ways in which Heartkeepers display their passion, but it's usually felt by the people they interact with and seen in the things they do in life. In practice, this means that two Heartkeepers can appear to live very different lives, but the basic element of their being, which is passion, is the same.

For instance, one Heartkeeper might focus solely on personal relationships and care much less about their work. These loving individuals direct their passion primarily toward the relationships they cultivate with people. On the other hand, some Heartkeepers will channel their love and passion through meaningful work, whether it's artistic expression, charity, activism, or any other endeavor that might touch other people's lives.

To embody the ways of this archetype, an individual has to ignite that passion in their heart. Those who possess it by default are truly blessed because life circumstances and experiences can cause a state of numbness in some people, where passion is hard to come by. To rekindle the flame of passion, you must seek out inspiration and try to feel as much as possible. Sometimes, deliberately exposing yourself to intense human emotions and inspiring personal stories can do the trick. Volunteering for causes, reading books, and forming close relationships are some of the best ways to expose yourself to these feelings.

However, finding your passion is just one part of the journey. To be a true Heartkeeper, you also need to know what to do with that passion.

You should channel it into creative hobbies and relationships, both of which will be made more vibrant when infused with passion. The ultimate objective should be to introduce meaning into your daily life, even if it's in small doses. The things you do shouldn't be mechanical tasks that you just want to get out of the way. At least a few aspects of your life should have a way of touching your heart on a deeper level. This way, you can feel as if you're doing more than just counting days. You should try to break up monotony and shake things up in any way you can because this is the only way you'll provide yourself with opportunities to find meaning.

Since this archetype is all about love and devotion, you can experiment with different objects of affection and caregiving. For instance, having a pet can enrich your life in ways you never expected. Devoting your time and energy to a living creature and letting yourself become emotionally attached is what the Heartkeeper is all about. A pet's bond can be incredibly powerful, but you shouldn't see it as a surrogate for human friendship and romantic connection. Consider it an overture to true emotional connection, which will make you more passionate, caring, and loving so that you'll open up to more meaningful connections in the future.

The Shadow of Emotional Confusion

Any archetype with such a pronounced central characteristic has the potential to veer off into the extreme. While it can be difficult to envision how such a loving archetype could have a shadow side, the Heartkeeper is not immune to human follies. Above all, the power and intensity of the Heartkeeper's emotions open up pitfalls in the form of uncontrollable emotional states that can lead to relationship problems, burnout, and poor decision-making.

For example, the Heartkeeper's feelings can be so intense that they completely overwhelm a person. Even though this archetype thrives on feelings, they can still feel too much and exhaust themselves mentally and emotionally. Learning how to articulate your feelings is a common antidote for this problem. This can be tricky because love doesn't leave a lot of room for rationality or analysis, and rightfully so. When it comes to loving a person, you don't need to understand why you love them, but you should have an idea of what you love about them.

Not only does this help to fully acknowledge your partner and make them feel embraced, but it'll also allow you to put some of your love into words. This is important because the essence of a relationship is to love someone else, not be obsessed with the abstract concept of love itself. That's how you truly see the person in front of you and shift focus from your own emotions and self-interest toward your loved one. Focusing on what you love instead of on how it makes you feel is also how you avoid becoming possessive, which is another common pitfall for the Heartkeeper.

Possessiveness begins with objectification, and it happens because you might begin to unconsciously see your relationship as a means to an end instead of an end in itself. Usually, the possessive Heartkeeper will treat their relationship as a refuge from personal fears, particularly rejection and loneliness. At that point, the relationship becomes a tool that the Heartkeeper uses instead of being the goal. In the simplest terms, your relationships, romantic or otherwise, are about the plural you, not the singular, and that's the distinction that some Heartkeepers might fail to make.

Unhinged passion, in the broadest sense, can also be the Heartkeeper's downfall. If it spirals out of control or is directed at the wrong thing, or both, the Heartkeeper's passion can lead an individual down some dark roads. For instance, the combination of misguided passion and an inability to handle rejection can make these individuals obsessive and invasive. The Heartkeeper's unhealthy obsessions can also be directed at causes, ideas, and much more, all of which will lead to some form of extremism that's never healthy.

In general, every Heartkeeper would do well to cultivate self-awareness and observe certain boundaries. They should set their own boundaries but also be mindful of those that other people have. Introspection, reflective exercises, and active listening can iron out most of these issues. The Heartkeeper needs to be especially mindful and heed the concerns of their loved ones when they voice certain disagreements or needs that might slightly conflict with this archetype's passions and desires.

The Superpower of Unyielding Love

The Heartkeeper's true superpower isn't necessarily in the intensity of the emotions felt but in the feelings that these individuals *can inspire* around them. Not only is their example inspirational and encouraging to the goodness in other people, but it can also infuse others with motivation. Passion is a powerful thing that can sometimes become contagious. When people see the Heartkeeper's passion for another person or some other pursuit, many of them will want a piece of that drive.

This archetype's powerful example might remind these people of their own repressed interests and ideas, motivating them to commit to these things so that they, too, could feel, at least, some of the passion they're seeing. The same applies to relationships, as the devoted and nurturing nature of the Heartkeeper can motivate people to take better care of their own relationships and perhaps fix some of the issues they've been neglecting. This is how the Heartkeeper cultivates joy, wherever they are, by enhancing their own emotional bonds and, by example, the bonds among others.

To cultivate this power within yourself is rather simple. You merely have to encourage yourself to engage in acts of devotion and expressions of love. These can be practical acts, but verbal expression can also be incredibly powerful under certain circumstances. A preexisting lack of passion and inner love can make this difficult for some people, so it's important to find ways to ignite passion in yourself first.

Unfortunately, people who don't love themselves can find it challenging to express love and devotion to others. That's why acts of self-love are so important if you are to become a true Heartkeeper. It seems counterintuitive at face value since this archetype is all about deep emotional connections and love for others, but it's true nonetheless. Just like bitterness and resentment, love begins within the individual, so you need to get right with yourself before you can start spreading joy to those around you. Most of the time, you'll radiate and project what you feel for yourself.

Another thing to note is that you shouldn't make it a priority to leave certain impressions on people. Passion has to come from within and be genuine. You shouldn't pursue it because you want to project a jolly image for the world and make yourself seem like something you're not.

Simply focus on finding love in the people and things you truly care about, chase what you're passionate about, and let the resulting inner peace and harmony spontaneously shine on the world. As long as you're content and feel true love in your heart, all you have to do is treat people with basic courtesy. They'll inevitably notice all of the goodness you've cultivated within yourself.

Practicing Gratitude and Rekindling Passion

In practical terms, cultivating your inner Heartkeeper has a lot to do with the kind of vibes that you seek out. Since this archetype is all about love and passion, it involves a lot of emotional work and reflection. Apart from seeking love in your life, you must also make sure that you're cherishing and growing the love that's already there. Nurturing acts and gestures of love are important for fostering other archetypes, but to be a true Heartkeeper, you have to truly feel that love. This means reflecting on your feelings, letting them blossom, and understanding them clearly.

As with many other archetypes, keeping a journal can be an excellent reflective activity to feed your Heartkeeper archetype. In particular, a journal of gratitude will help you articulate your feelings for the loved ones in your life. By outlining what you're grateful for and why, you'll put your feelings into words as much as these human emotions allow. It's a way to drown out all the background noise and confusion that so often obfuscate such feelings. Focus your journal entries specifically on the people that you love, and try to identify as many ways in which they enrich your life as you can.

Gratitude can and should also be addressed to yourself and your life. You can practice all sorts of gratitude rituals that feature forms of self-love, with an emphasis on being mindful of what you're grateful for. Writing a sort of love letter to yourself might clarify the things that make you passionate and remind you that love should flow in both directions. This can also be a rather creative exercise that makes you look at certain things in a different light since most people aren't used to writing love letters to themselves or addressing themselves from that perspective.

In general, you should pursue creative outlets in the broadest sense because this is one of the best ways to uncover hidden passions and stoke that flame within you. Poetry, painting, and music are some of the most powerful conduits for human passion, and they have the potential to inspire profound new feelings, even in people who've never considered themselves particularly creative. While you can certainly acquire the skills through practice, these creative outlets aren't dependent on creating the next artistic masterpiece. Instead, their power is in the fact that they allow the inner contents of your heart and soul to flow out unfiltered.

Regardless of the quality of your work, art will enable you to express yourself in ways that you never thought possible. The words you can summon in regular conversations tend to be subject to all sorts of filters and interference, both conscious and unconscious. When you're alone in a personal space, with no distractions around, your mind will likely work very differently, especially when you commit yourself to a creative process. Remember that creative outlets come in many forms that go beyond art. If you feel that you lack passion for the things in your life, try to take on as many creative endeavors as you can until something gives.

Chapter 9: The Visionary – Architect of the Future

The Visionary archetype is an unyielding creative force that turns concepts and ideas into real-world applications. Based on the likes of the creator and magician archetypes, the Visionary is a crafty, intelligent trailblazer with an incredible capacity for innovation. This is certainly one of the most fascinating archetypes out there, and it possesses more than one kind of depth. Individuals exhibiting this archetype can be vastly different from one another, having unique interests and skills with a powerful imagination as the common denominator. This chapter will analyze the most creative archetype and help you figure out how you can cultivate such thinking for the betterment of yourself and those around you.

The Visionary is the architect of the future.[19]

Archetype Profile

The Visionary is an archetype that fosters forward-thinking and creativity above all else. These innate qualities make the archetype incredibly versatile and capable of taking on a plethora of tasks, but the overarching themes are usually innovation and invention. This archetype also benefits from a deeply rooted supply of inspiration that resembles passion in that it's a powerful driver, but it actually comes from a place of creativity. That's because the Visionary's mind is an endless reel of ideas that never stop flowing, allowing them to come up with new solutions and look at things from a novel angle.

Such creative thinking enables the Visionary to find the way forward in most situations and, in practice, makes this archetype appear driven, passionate, and borderline obsessive at times. When the Visionary becomes consumed by an idea, there is hardly a force in the world that can stop them from seeing it through. Visionaries' ideas are particularly powerful when they revolve around solving a problem and changing an established paradigm.

Needless to say, the Visionary is one of the most powerful and impactful archetypes that exist in humanity. These are the people who push the envelope and redefine what is possible, allowing civilizations to leap forward and break new ground. When reality has too many constraints, Visionaries will create new realities whose inception begins in their imagination. This archetype is also usually fortified with confidence, at least in their ideas. If a Visionary has spent enough time perfecting such an idea, they will build up an unwavering belief in that concept. This trait can lead to a few pitfalls but also imbues an individual with the potential for greatness.

It's not uncommon for the Visionary to leave a lasting legacy based on the work they do. That legacy is an impetus for a lot of Visionaries, but it's not always the primary motivation behind their work. A Visionary who's committed to science might be more inclined to obsess over their complicated work and its potential results, not thinking too much about the consequences that work might have for the endurance of their name or personal glory. However, Visionaries can also be artists, athletes, and much more, sometimes finding themselves in competitive fields where legacy is a powerful motive. It's not necessarily a question of ego and vanity, as a healthy Visionary will be driven primarily by the rewarding feeling of having pushed a boundary rather than by being celebrated. It just so happens that a vision or creation that truly breaks new ground will almost always result in a lasting legacy, whether the Visionary wants it or not.

One thing that the Visionary fears is mediocrity. Visionary people will push themselves as far as possible to ensure they're performing at their maximum. While they can often be unconventional or quirky, they tend to have a strong work ethic that leaves little room for anything other than their work. Strangely enough, it's not uncommon for Visionaries to struggle with their finances, even if they work all day. This is the price that some Visionaries pay for treading into unexplored territories and trying to go against the grain, working obsessively on personal projects that might seem like a waste of time to others until they're not.

Embodying Vision

To embody the characteristics of the Visionary, you need two key ingredients. The first is to turn your thoughts to the future, and the second is to embrace bold, innovative ideas. If you feel these are foreign concepts, the best first step is to simply immerse yourself in similar ideas floating around from other thinkers. Start analyzing current trends and what they might lead to while researching all things novel, bold, and innovative within your sphere of interest.

If the things you research tickle your mind, you'll likely start getting a few ideas of your own, even if they're just modifications of the things you've read about. In fact, a lot of great ideas start this way. You must find ways to tap into your creative potential while developing a future-focused mindset. The exact ways in which you'll do this depend entirely on your interests and approach, but it usually starts with new hobbies.

A hobby can help you tinker with ideas without investing too much time or money or putting a strain on other areas of your life until something clicks. You should develop a methodical approach that focuses on building a skill, experimenting with it, and exploring new ideas with small initial steps while constantly pushing your boundaries. If you want to truly commit to your vision, there will come a time when you'll have to fully embrace the idea and take decisive steps in your life. The winning strategy is to go slow at first, test the waters, and build yourself a jumping board before that day comes.

You must stimulate your hunger for more information and knowledge while building a goal-oriented mindset. Being goal-oriented means playing the long game and not letting momentary setbacks or distractions pull you from your path. It's the art of focus where you'll keep your main vision clearly in your crosshairs at all times while also being able to work on the tasks currently at hand. Visualizing that long-term destination despite all current factors is the essence of being a Visionary. Still, you have to balance that vision with practicality and give your endeavor a structure by breaking it up into actionable steps.

You can give yourself a handy reminder by writing your vision down in your journal. For instance, actionable steps can be your weekly or monthly milestones that all feed into the long-term goal, even if that goal is years away. The important thing is to have some picture of the journey ahead and establish a thread that you'll follow. A goal-oriented mindset will help you to persevere when one of your short-term steps proves tricky and grinds your efforts down to a halt. This will inevitably happen, but if you keep your goal firmly in mind, you'll be able to improvise and adapt.

The Shadow of Obsession

With such a keen, intense mind, there are a lot of things that can go wrong. One of the Visionary's greatest frenemies is perfectionism. This obsessive approach is what enables some Visionaries to change the world, yet it's also the reason why some of them will fail to deliver practical results, even if they're working off a genius idea. It can be difficult for these Visionaries to figure out when their efforts should cease, especially if they're completely indifferent to external feedback and criticism.

In a similar vein, the vision itself can become a trap for this archetype if it envelops their life entirely. This is especially true for grand ideas that go way beyond the conventions of what's considered possible or practical. In the relentless pursuit of such an idea, the Visionary can completely neglect the rest of their life, relationships, and even reason itself. If the Visionary goes out to fight windmills while everything else in their life crumbles, things can get very ugly for them and everyone around them.

History has known quite a few examples of great inventors or artists living such a life and eventually breaking through to their goal. However, these stories are remembered for their eventual successes, not for the herculean, self-destructive manner in which the Visionary lived. When an obsessive Visionary abandons everything except their vision, lives a life resembling that of a hermit, and finally succeeds, the facts of their harsh life become historical trivia. If they don't succeed, their misery will be forgotten along with their work. In the rarest of cases, ideas can be so far ahead of their time that the Visionary dies in poverty while their idea lives on, etching their name into the pages of history long after they are gone.

Overall, the shadow tends to overtake the Visionary when the archetype loses its grounding and becomes overly idealistic. Lofty goals with no realistic thinking will inevitably struggle to produce results, which will produce a lot of frustration and pain for the perfectionist Visionary. The chase itself is the reward for a lot of Visionaries, but it will be a love-hate relationship at best – and painful personal ruin at worst.

To avoid losing yourself in your dreams, you must strike a balance between allowing your imagination to do its thing and keeping a semblance of control through critical thinking. Still, when Visionaries get obsessed with an idea, being critical and objective can become incredibly difficult, especially if the individual in question is an artist and not a scientist. This is where constructive external criticism and feedback come into play.

Visionaries can benefit immensely from maintaining at least one or two close relationships with people whom they completely trust. Ideally, that person will be respectful of the Visionary's mission and talent, but they'll also care for them on a personal level. This emotional guide who knows the Visionary intimately will understand how to foster their talents while also making sure they don't veer off course and take the path of self-destruction.

Mentors, dear friends, family members, and romantic partners can all fulfill this role, and they don't necessarily have to fully understand the work that their Visionary friend is doing. The Visionary must allow their vision to run free, and they must be persistent, yet they must also remain as pragmatic, practical, and realistic as humanly possible. If striking this kind of balance is difficult for you, don't hesitate to seek support.

Creativity and Forethought as Superpowers

The Visionary's superpower is the mind. This archetype achieves groundbreaking thought by easily thinking outside the box and pushing beyond conventional boundaries. Unusual thinking patterns combined with high creativity enable the Visionary to see things from angles and perspectives that don't even occur to most other people. Quite often, the Visionary will see solutions and possibilities where others see nothing, and they might even see these things where others see an impenetrable wall.

They possess a signature ability to see ahead of the game, and this foresight is often the reason why some Visionaries are seen as either mad or as being way ahead of their time. Unfortunately, the latter is often realized by the masses only years or decades after the Visionary is gone. This is especially true of artists because their work doesn't have a practical, scientific application that can immediately change the course of civilization. The legacy of artistic works comes from the public's ability to appreciate that art. Truly visionary art will have a tendency to become more relevant as time goes by. This is what eventually returns the artist's name to the spotlight as the masses finally unlock and absorb the full extent of the artistry contained within. Only then will people unearth that which only the visionary artist and a few other people understood at the time of creation.

Artists, in particular, have amazing foresight.[30]

In general, the ideas that occur to the Visionary are bold and have the potential to shape the future, which can manifest on various levels of the human experience. Not every Visionary archetype will be embodied in a famous inventor or artist or even in an inventor or artist who fails. Some

Visionaries are content to remain within their personal circle and manifest their visions in the lives of a select few people. Coming up with great solutions to personal problems or taking your friends on an incredibly creative adventure are examples of some more grounded ways in which your Visionary archetype can emerge.

The primary method of harnessing your Visionary archetype is fostering the talents that you have and letting your creativity run wild. Any idea that's fundamentally transformative in at least one human life can be considered visionary. If you can articulate those ideas and inspire other people, even if it's just in your small community, you'll be tapping into this archetype. Pursue creativity at every opportunity, embrace cooperation with others when needed, and work on your resilience. These three factors will allow you to conceive ideas, seek out the necessary external support, and persevere through setbacks as you work toward making those ideas a reality.

Visualization and Action

On the practical side of things, the thought process of cultivating your innate creativity will be the way of harnessing the Visionary archetype. You should put special emphasis on making your goals future-oriented and ambitious yet feasible. The best way to construct such goals is to brainstorm and engage in deep analysis, writing down as many aspects of the plan as possible. When you put the plan on paper, it'll be easier for you to observe the full picture with impartial eyes and see how well the different moving parts of the plan come together into a holistic, feasible vision.

Every Visionary should have something similar to a vision board detailing their ideas, goals, and hopes. A vision board, also called a dream board, is simply a collection of images, affirmations, inspirational quotes, ideas, and other bits and pieces that represent your dreams and wishes for the future. Your vision board can be made on a bulletin board, resembling a collage hanging on your wall. Part of your vision board's purpose will be to outline your vision and help you make plans. On the other hand, it'll also serve as a constant reminder that provides you with inspiration and motivation to continue chasing an idea.

If the idea of a vision board feels too passive, you can complement or replace it with a so-called action board. This would be a more action-oriented collage focused on specific tasks and detailing your progress on those tasks. Since the Visionary usually relies on one all-encompassing vision or central idea, it's best to use both of these boards to articulate that vision. This is because ideas can sometimes be a bit on the abstract side, and breaking it down into specific, practical steps might take away some of the idea's visionary aspects. Rather than choosing between focusing on that which is practical or a certain ambitious idea, you should focus on both.

The practice of visualization can also help you further align your vision with your actions. Visualization is essential and comes naturally to those whose Visionary archetype is strong and clean, but it's a highly useful practice that can help anyone who's pursuing a certain goal. This is a simple mental technique that revolves around formulating clear, powerful mental images of a future outcome, particularly the end goal of your vision.

Visualizing your success can boost confidence and help you stay focused on the long-term goal, increasing your resilience to setbacks. When you visualize the materialization of your goal, try to also imagine your journey toward that point. As clearly as you can, cultivate a mental image of the steps you'll be taking to make each leap toward your goal. This will help you make sure that those steps make sense of the goal in question and that you're on the right trajectory.

Chapter 10: The Disruptor – Witty Instigator of Transformation

The Disruptor is based on Jung's trickster archetype, also commonly known as the jester or joker. This archetype has a fair bit of common ground with a number of other archetypes but puts a very unique spin on its amalgamation of traits. The Disruptor pushes boundaries similarly to the Rebel and enjoys instigating transformation like a couple of others, but this archetype does these things in a way that's highly characteristic and unmistakable. This chapter will acquaint you with the wittiest archetype and all its strengths and quirks.

The Disruptor.[21]

Archetype Profile

People with all sorts of archetypes can have a sense of humor, but the Disruptor uses it for more than just making people laugh. This archetype brings to the table a brand of witty provocation that aims to poke holes in narratives, challenge authority, question conventions, and push boundaries. Disruptors can be quite funny, but above all, they aim to be clever. They are in their element when their provocative attitude and humor are backed up with actual knowledge and information that enables them to make strong arguments through comedy. Failing to present useful information, the Disruptor can become frivolous and directionless.

The Disruptor is the kind of person who accepts and embraces the absurdities and paradoxes of the human condition – *and makes light of those facts.* They particularly enjoy exposing the hypocrisies of others, especially those who take themselves too seriously or assume to possess the moral high ground. When someone tries to build a deceptive narrative or push an agenda through moral grandstanding or any kind of manipulative demagogy, the Disruptor will take great pleasure in taking a sledgehammer to that person's constructs.

Even if they aren't acting in a moral capacity or addressing someone's malicious intent, Disruptors will still enjoy pushing boundaries and just having a good. This is a fun-loving archetype that lives for the present moment and never takes things too seriously, especially their own self. The Disruptor has no problem making jokes at their own expense and indulging in some good, old, self-deprecating humor, but they will also expect others to be able to take a joke. Assuming that they don't give in to their shadow side, Disruptors will generally bring a joyous atmosphere to gatherings and make quick work of purging any negative vibes from the situation.

Disruptors are often misunderstood because a lot of people, at first glance, might consider them irresponsible, frivolous, and unable to take anything seriously. This can be true of some Disruptors who haven't found their balance yet, but more often than not, the Disruptor can be surprisingly insightful. When people scratch beneath the surface, Disruptors can present a wealth of knowledge and understanding that can illuminate important truths via a seemingly carefree attitude.

The light-hearted Disruptor fears boredom and an uneventful life. For this archetype, losing the ability to laugh at life and take challenges in stride is a nightmare scenario that they'll try to avoid at all costs. Disruptors thrive on change and live to provoke transformations in worldly circumstances and other people. Their ideal life is subject to change and novelty while featuring plenty of creativity. They are playful, irreverent, and subversive. The Disruptor will subvert systems and norms, but they'll also subvert the expectations of others by pulling an ace out of their sleeve and surprising everyone when they least expect.

Disruptors can make a powerful impression on others with their unique combination of traits and attitudes. They can provoke others into positive, constructive change by shining a spotlight on the absurdity of their problems. They have a way of helping other people see their problems as less terrifying and more manageable. This ability to make light of anything can spark completely new ways of thinking in people's minds and make them see things from a fresh new perspective. In essence, the Disruptor's life mission is to infiltrate the hearts of people through laughter, sparking important conversations in the process and, ultimately, triggering change.

Embodying Transformation

Embodying the Disruptor can be a bit difficult if you don't have a natural knack for humor, particularly the kind that's able to poke fun at serious matters. A person can't simply become funny overnight, but you can always start small with simple mental adjustments. For instance, the art of finding silver linings is a great gateway toward developing a sense of humor. The trick is to make a mental shift toward positivity and keep your mind from obsessing over the negative aspects of a situation. The more positive your thinking is, the more likely you are to develop a sense of humor.

However, the most important ways in which you can tap into the Disruptor's energy are largely similar to those of the Rebel. You'll need to cultivate creativity and out-of-box thinking so that you can come up with solutions to back up your second-guessing of authority with alternative offers. The key to successful and productive disruptions is to tear down the status quo and offer something that you feel people should adopt instead of the established norm. If you just tear things down and walk away, people will quickly start seeing you as a nuisance more than an instigator of change.

To embody the Disruptor, you must also learn to embrace discomfort. There is no way for the Disruptor to provoke people and push them to leave their comfort zones without being used to discomfort in their own lives. You should see discomfort as an opportunity for growth and transformation and call it your home. Making everyone uncomfortable in the interest of positive change is a healthy Disruptor's signature move, so you must learn to operate smoothly when things get unstable. To accept discomfort as an opportunity, you should see it as the key driver of change instead of something to endure until it passes.

Work on developing your resilience and challenge yourself at every chance to grow a thicker skin. With enough practice, you can get used to adversity and put yourself at a significant advantage before you begin provoking the powers that be. For would-be Disruptors, one of the best ways to do this is to purposely seek out opposing views or anything else that annoys you and expose yourself to these things gradually and consistently enough to develop tolerance. Once you become immune to insult and provocation, you'll be ready to pose the trickiest questions and push people to their limits.

The Shadow of Chaos

If you harbor a pronounced Disruptor archetype within your heart, you must beware that it doesn't cast its shadow on you. If that happens, the Disruptor can take away your ability to take anything seriously and make you irresponsible. The Disruptor's shadow side can also manifest as an overwhelming cynicism that can take a dark turn as it spirals beyond dark humor and enters the territory of despair, discouragement, and a complete collapse of motivation to do anything worthwhile. A degree of cynicism can act as a shield and help you question authority, but too much of it will eventually get you to question whether there's a purpose in anything, including life itself.

The shadowy Disruptor is an irresponsible individual without a clear focus who simply lashes out. For them, humor is a means of escape, not communication. They don't really want to get to the crux of the problem and motivate others toward positive change. Instead, they just want to tear everything down, including people, usually because they're feeling directionless in their lives. A directionless Disruptor can wreak havoc on their own life and leave a trail of destruction everywhere they go. Even if they have a great laugh while they're at it, this kind of lifestyle will inevitably lead to ruin.

The Disruptor can learn to offset their destructive tendencies with thoughtful consideration in many ways. One of the best methods is to become more forward-thinking in the way they approach situations. The Disruptor is a type of person who enjoys living for today; this can be a bit more difficult than it seems. Outlining goals and planning ahead can help you develop a more future-oriented mindset as a force of habit.

If you have an innate desire to provoke people, you should try to do so only after you've considered the ways in which your provocations can serve a constructive purpose. Do your best to analyze situations objectively and figure out what kind of positive results can be achieved if you act provocatively in a given situation. Think about any potential lessons that the people involved might learn or the mistakes they might realize once you start disrupting the narrative. If you're finding it difficult to imagine a positive outcome, that's probably because there won't be one. In such situations, being more careful and restrained is usually the better approach. This is how a Disruptor can act with consideration and thoughtfulness instead of defaulting to causing chaos.

The Power of Directed Disruption

The Disruptor's rebelliousness and the lighthearted way in which they go about it are the essence of this archetype's strength. Their superpowers lie in their ability to take challenges in stride and sniff out nonsense that should be questioned. The Disruptor is particularly dominant when he or she is armed with facts, knowledge, and strong arguments that they keep under wraps until it's time for confrontation. They are one of the most difficult archetypes to manipulate and fool because they're naturally skeptical and always feel an itch to poke fun.

To harness this power in a healthy way, the Disruptor should take care not to become too self-absorbed. If you're going to go down the road with this archetype, you should do your best to retain a semblance of modesty and accept the fact that you won't always be the smartest person in the room. As much as you might want to challenge authority and flip narratives upside down through your wit, there will indeed be moments when you'd be well-advised to tone it down and open your mind.

The Disruptor's goal shouldn't be to tear things down just for their personal amusement. Instead, you should aim to spark creativity in yourself and those around you while fostering innovation and encouraging positive changes. Disruption will often be a legitimate means to that end, but it shouldn't become an end in itself. You should embrace every challenge with a lighthearted attitude and use your humor to question everything, including yourself and your own opinions.

In general, the Disruptor benefits from a lot of the same advice that the Rebel needs to hear. Instead of giving in to destructive impulses, both of these archetypes need to identify a cause that's worth upholding and cherish their moral integrity. When you stick to your principles and pursue a worthy goal, your humorous defiance will shine its best light and inspire others to follow along. Beyond just humor and snarky remarks, the Disruptor should act as an example and profess a coherent message that people can get behind. This is how the Disruptor becomes a force for good and constructively utilizes their talents.

Being unconventional is important for most Disruptors. They're especially unconventional in their methods and are generally glad to embrace a challenge, allowing them to test their quirky solutions and resilience. The Disruptor has the strength to laugh in the face of hardship, but they do so to fortify themselves and stay on the path towards their goal. Their humor doesn't serve as a means of escaping reality or brushing off things that matter.

When the Disruptor criticizes and deconstructs outdated assumptions, traditions, or rules, they don't do so to escape responsibility or stir up trouble just for fun. They do this because they genuinely feel that an unconventional approach might yield better results, and they don't mind making that clear. This is why the Disruptor is so conducive to innovation when they're well-intentioned and goal-oriented.

Finding Things to Disrupt

Your main focus should be knowing when you should use your disruptive energy and dial it down. The good Disruptor will have sound judgment and observe some basic principles of common sense in their conduct. No matter your circumstances, there will be people and situations that deserve your respect. The way you carry yourself in those moments will determine the kind of Disruptor you'll be. However, respect doesn't mean that you have to suppress your humor and be something you're not.

The way to keep your Disruptor archetype under some basic constraints will be similar to the Rebel archetype. You'll want to analyze your life and identify those areas where you feel that you're feeling repressed, especially if the pressure is coming from traditional thinking and established norms that are ripe for criticism. Just like the Rebel, the Disruptor will approach these situations critically and get to the root of the problem that's making them feel trapped.

The differences in the way that these two archetypes respond to such situations begin with the way they voice their concerns. The Rebel will usually engage in a sort of face-value defiance where they get right to the point as clearly as they can. On the other hand, Disruptors tend to err on the side of creativity, coming up with clever ways to upset the status quo and gradually push things in the desired direction. The Disruptor will rely on trickery and strategy, taking their time to come up with a creative solution.

To incite change in creative ways, you'll have to make sure that you're not being impulsive. Disruptors will usually bide their time and start out with a few wisecracks at certain intervals, cleverly hinting at ways in which the situation should be changed or improved. The humor provides a surface layer of friendliness and lighthearted banter that's cleverly balanced between making a point and not rushing straight into conflict. Making people laugh is a way of disarming them, so if you can simultaneously make your superiors laugh and hint at the fact that you'd like a promotion, you'll have performed a signature Disruptor move.

Always try to experiment with various creative solutions and do your best to stay subtle. You want to be slightly provocative, humorous, and not openly confrontational, at least not until it becomes necessary. The Disruptor isn't the kind of person who beats around the bush or is afraid of getting to the point. Rather, they have a keen sense of other people's buttons and know exactly how many they should push in a given situation. In extreme situations, the Disruptor might have to openly provoke and incite some chaos, but in most daily interactions, a more restrained approach will do the trick.

If you have a natural sense of humor, you can try using it in as many situations as possible to cultivate this aspect of your character. Disruptors are especially adept at using it to address difficult topics, which requires a lot of tact and sensitivity. It's a skill that can be developed, but you have to make sure that you don't lack empathy. This is because you'll need to have a solid picture of how people might react to humor when certain topics are being discussed.

A common rule of thumb is that you shouldn't take charge and rush straight into dark humor. Instead, you should let other people speak first and carefully analyze their demeanor so that you can gauge their level of sensitivity and current emotional state. If your instincts are clean and accurate, you'll be able to identify opportunities where a funny quip might be not just acceptable but *endearing and uplifting*. Humor is a game of finesse and balance, which can't really be taught. You simply have to practice and observe how people react until you create your perfect formula.

Chapter 11: The Wise One – Keeper of Knowledge

Inspired by Jung's sage archetype, which goes by many other names in psychology circles, the Wise One is a powerful archetype that's primarily focused on knowledge. Since knowledge is one of the most important tools driving the wheels of civilization, the Wise One is an essential archetype that transforms the lives of individuals, communities, and humanity as a whole. In this final chapter, you'll learn about the archetype that nurtures the human thirst for knowledge, wisdom, and truth.

The Wise One is the keeper of knowledge.[22]

Archetype Profile

A person with a pronounced Wise One archetype usually possesses a deeper understanding of the world and its affairs, always craves to learn more, and often makes it a mission to guide others toward wisdom. Some of the Wise Ones might be more withdrawn, introverted, and concerned with their own world, not going out of their way to teach and mentor other people. Even so, they still tend to make excellent advisors and guides if someone engages them with questions and seeks their support.

The Wise One is characterized by a keen mind empowered by clarity of thought and a highly analytical view of the larger processes at play. As such, this archetype has a knack for grasping the bigger picture and making sense of seemingly disparate bits of information that make up a larger puzzle. Wise Ones will unlock insights that transcend the more obvious, immediate information thanks to their ability to look beyond the proverbial tree and peer deep into the entire forest.

Where others might get hung up on details and miss what these details tell them about the grand scheme of things, the Wise One will see right through the surface level and easily decipher the essence of a problem. The Wise One's understanding of the world goes way beyond the cataloging of individual facts, focusing instead on the whole truth. This is an important distinction that the Wise One makes, and it marks the nuanced difference between wisdom and knowledge.

Wise Ones apply the same principle when they act in the capacity of mentors and advisors. When they teach, they want to make sure that the learner arrives at the crux of the issue and holistically processes the information that the Wise One imparts. They teach with the goal of understanding and wisdom in mind, not to share shallow information that does little more than pique someone's interest.

The introspection that the Wise One is capable of is something that a lot of other archetypes chase in order to live a more balanced life. This archetype's wisdom rarely allows for follies, such as arrogance. The Wise One tends to be self-aware as introspection comes naturally to their insightful and analytical nature. Just as Wise Ones glean deeper insights from understanding the world, they can look at themselves with the same depth and figure out their personal issues. Like anyone else, the Wise One isn't infallible, but this archetype possesses the clarity of thought and the sort of calmness that makes them less likely to succumb to delusions.

The Wise One's calm demeanor is matched only by their thoughtfulness, making it highly unlikely for these individuals to be impulsive, irrational, and reckless. Cautious analysis is the name of the game for this archetype, and they apply the same mentality when they engage in mentorship. Their analytical approach doesn't necessitate judgment, but the Wise One will definitely call a spade a spade if the situation requires it. The Wise One is usually philosophical and insightful, with everyone around them providing valuable perspectives that can help others get on a path to wisdom on their own journeys toward the truth.

Embodying Knowledge

The depth of knowledge that the Wise One possesses will almost always result in humility. They often know a lot about the world, but their vast knowledge doesn't serve to feed and inflate their ego or denigrate others. On the contrary, their knowledge only reinforces their understanding that there is so much more to learn and that, in the grand scheme of things, their knowledge is limited. This awareness is the essence of learning, and it is what drives the Wise One to seek out new knowledge in perpetuity.

The Wise One's humility is usually accompanied by wise patience and a willingness to listen. Their thirst for knowledge is often manifested in how they interact with other people who have their own wisdom to teach. Whenever someone speaks and shares their knowledge, the Wise One will patiently listen and absorb any new information they might extract from the conversation. This archetype welcomes every opportunity to learn and is more interested in accumulating knowledge than debating or arguing a point. If and when the Wise One does engage in constructive debate, they will do so with tact, patience, and respect. More importantly, any debate will serve as just another chance to broaden their horizons and examine new points of view.

Wise Ones also understand that knowledge comes from more than just literature. They're certainly in their element when they're reading a book that fascinates them, but these individuals will also learn through life experiences, real-world observations, insightful conversations, and listening to as many perspectives as they can. One of the most important lessons that this archetype teaches is that knowledge comes in all forms and from countless sources, sometimes where you least expect it. Keeping an open mind and being on the lookout for this knowledge is one of the surest ways to attain wisdom.

If you want to embody the studiousness of the Wise One, you'd do well to adopt the traits mentioned above. You must first become patient and calm in the things you do, assuming that this is something you struggle with. If you're stressed out and spend most of your waking hours constrained by an emotional and intellectual tunnel vision, you have to find ways to take back the reins. Meditation, yoga, physical exercise, and anything else that helps you unwind and expel excess energy will be of great help.

To alter the way in which you learn, you have to change the way you carry yourself. Seek out knowledge beyond reading and try to interact with people who exhibit the traits of the Wise One. Prepare yourself to listen and become an observer rather than a participant or leader in every situation. Being active and having leadership potential are both great traits, but if it's higher wisdom and knowledge you seek, then you have to learn how to occasionally take a backseat as well. Practice active listening and mindfulness so that you're completely present in every situation, and make your brain as absorbent as possible. To be the Wise One is to carefully observe, analyze, contemplate, and absorb the world around you, which is what often makes this archetype inwardly oriented and introverted.

The Shadow of the Impractical Genius

The Wise One's struggles often stem from the need to balance their intellectual pursuits and practical necessities. The Wise One can become aloof and overly involved in their inner world, to a point where it becomes difficult to take action or reach practical solutions to problems. When the Wise One's shadow envelops you, learning can become its own trap by getting you too caught up in the details of what you're studying. While knowledge is an important part of the pursuit of wisdom, it's a good idea to ensure that it doesn't become your only goal. Knowledge should serve at least some practical purpose – if for no other reason, simply because life itself is just as practical as it is theoretical. If not more.

Knowledge is important to the Wise One.*

When an individual becomes overly intellectual, they can also lose their ability to enjoy the little moments in life and derive joy from the things they learn. The thirst for knowledge should involve a degree of passion and revolve around more than just accumulating information and breaking through intellectual milestones. Wise Ones have to grant themselves some license to get lost in their world of learning, but it's important not to become detached from practical realities.

Another area that the shadowy Wise One can often neglect is the emotional side of life. This archetype can sometimes have a tendency to become too hardened and even emotionally numb if their over-intellectualization and analytical mind start to deconstruct emotions from a purely intellectual perspective. This can be a major problem if the Wise One wishes to assume the role of a mentor or guide for other people. To be a good teacher requires the ability to communicate on an emotional level, not just impart knowledge. It can also involve empathy and some allowance for the dimensions of human interaction that aren't entirely subject to intellectualism.

The answer is to remain grounded in the more basic levels of the human experience by cultivating empathy and practicality. You can achieve this balance by making sure that some of your interactions with people revolve around sharing the little moments, even if they seem frivolous. Not every minute spent together has to emphasize intellectual exchanges. Sometimes, it will do you well to just have fun and let yourself unwind in the company of someone you care about.

You should also make sure that you have goals in life, especially practical, short-term ones. Your overall, long-term goal in life can be to learn as much as possible. Even though this goal is somewhat vague, on a weekly or monthly basis, you should set some goals that produce tangible results. The best way to keep yourself grounded is to maintain a journal about these goals and track your progress as a reminder that you're taking action and getting things done in the real world, not just in your mind. Another great way to stay practical is to develop real-world skills, which can be related to your day job or a crafty hobby.

Tapping into the Power of the Intellect

The Wise One's greatest superpower is the archetype's ability to maintain clarity of thought and observe the world through a thirst for knowledge instead of emotional impulses and reactive mindsets. To tap into this archetype's strengths, you have to take control of your thoughts and keep your mind clear. Excess energy is a common polluter of the mental process, so you should start by finding ways to expel it. The best way to do this is through something constructive, creative, or physical.

When you decompress, you'll inevitably become calmer, more stable, and patient. At this point, you can start altering your schedule to allow more time for reading and studying. As you take more control over your life and begin learning more than ever before, you should start enhancing your critical thinking skills. The art of critical thinking has been covered earlier in this book, but it's especially important for the Wise One archetype. Without critical thought, the value of the information you absorb will be considerably diminished. Everyone can amass facts in their memory, but it takes a particular way of thinking to properly analyze and integrate these facts in the interest of truth.

An important thing to understand about critical thinking is that it's not entirely natural for people. As evolved and self-aware as they are, human beings still tend to default to instinct in most situations that don't require immediate problem-solving. To think critically at all times and evaluate every bit of information that comes your way is a skill that has to be learned, honed, and perfected. The Wise One's patience, calm, and thoughtfulness play key roles in their ability to think critically.

Apart from learning the truths of the world, wisdom also comes from examining and understanding your own life. Most Wise Ones turn their focus inward, just as much as they immerse themselves in the outside world. This is why they often turn to meditation, yoga, religion, spirituality, and all manner of intellectual or spiritual pursuits that expand their minds. They realize that to truly understand the world, one must also know themselves and be in a perpetual state of soul-searching.

All of these things will require reflection and time. Finding ways to strike a balance between relentless intellectual pursuit and the necessities of regular life is a common theme in the Wise One's struggles. They usually find a way to achieve it, though, because their thirst for knowledge is a powerful driver that propels them forward and helps them find ways to accommodate their intellectual cravings.

The Wise One's true power can perhaps be summarized in their love for knowledge, which is something that not everyone possesses. To become wise, you have to feel this thirst on a fundamental level, somewhere deep inside your soul. If you find that difficult and are prone to intellectual laziness, you must first find ways to unclog your mind and rekindle your curiosity. Start by finding topics that you're interested in and begin studying them right away. If you're lucky to find something you're deeply interested in, then your passion will certainly ignite when you dig deep enough.

Trading Time for Wisdom

This isn't an unbreakable universal rule, but the unfortunate reality is that most people who rush through life with packed schedules and little personal time will find it difficult to attend to matters of wisdom. A lot of people nowadays don't even find the time to accumulate plain information by reading, let alone explore the depths of true wisdom and spend time in reflection and philosophy. The simple truth is that this is what true wisdom usually demands. You must reflect, introspect, keep a journal, and search your soul on top of reading and learning about the world.

Wisdom is something that comes with years and cannot be acquired overnight via a simple recipe. Each individual's journey toward true wisdom can have unique twists and turns depending on life circumstances, past experiences, and issues to be resolved. It goes without saying that you must learn as much as you can and study things like philosophy. You're also encouraged to read spiritual texts because wisdom often has a spiritual dimension that goes beyond the intellectual and the scientific. Each day, you should allocate time to reflect on the lessons you've learned recently or in the distant past. Whether through meditation, journaling, or anything else, you need to spend time with your thoughts and commit to them.

You should also seek out opportunities to impart these lessons to others in your community. Guidance and mentorship are important parts of life for many Wise Ones because the act of teaching others feeds right back into their own process of learning and growth. Still, the most important thing is to practice patience, thoughtfulness, and a level of calm that allows you to stop for a moment and peer into the deeper layers of the world and its reality as a whole. The most important steps on your journey toward wisdom and enlightenment might be all about changing your attitudes toward yourself and the world, more so than reading and gathering information. Acknowledge the limitations of your knowledge, adopt humility and thoughtfulness, and open your mind to the truth at all times, even when it's uncomfortable.

The pursuit of wisdom might require you to drastically restructure your days and free up parts of your schedule. Apart from reflective practices and philosophy studies, each day should also have some time allocated to other intellectual pursuits. To become a Wise One, you don't have to absorb all worldly knowledge over time, but you do have to dig deeper into the things you choose to learn. You should focus on a few interests and stay in your lane in terms of topics, but commit to them and learn as much as possible.

You must also remember to indulge your creativity through whatever outlets seem appropriate to your interests and skills. Becoming wise doesn't necessarily entail becoming a great artist, but creativity, in the broadest sense, encourages reflection and self-exploration. Whatever method of expression you use will help you grow intellectually and spiritually over time.

Conclusion

The archetypes you've learned about throughout this book represent a collection of human inclinations, traits, behaviors, mentalities, and much more. When put together, these archetypes paint a picture of humanity as a whole, with its many diversities, talents, blessings, quirks, and follies. There's a bit of every archetype in everyone, and you've hopefully been able to identify which of the archetypes are more dominant in your own personality.

As you've seen, archetypes can also be encouraged and cultivated to a great extent to unlock the hidden strengths that lie dormant within you. The point to take home is that the description or characteristics of these archetypes shouldn't be used to categorize yourself rigidly into one or two archetypes and forget the rest. On the contrary, the idea behind the archetypes is to help you realize and discover new things about yourself and, just as importantly, to figure out which areas of your life and character you want to strengthen or how your existing archetypes can be improved.

Not everyone can embody every archetype completely, but they can certainly get close. People do have the capacity to change their attitudes, habits, mentalities, interests, and all the other things that are influenced by psychological archetypes. Learning about the archetypes that you respect yet don't immediately recognize within yourself shouldn't be discouraging. It should inspire you to outgrow the constraints of what you once thought to be your definitions and realize that life offers plenty of opportunities for you to evolve.

Furthermore, the archetypes you've learned about can serve as your guide in understanding people better. Hopefully, you've recognized how some of these archetypes might be present in the people you care about. You've seen how each archetype, no matter how impressive its traits, has its shadow side. This says something about the fallibility of people and the fact that anyone can lose their way and make mistakes.

Whether you've recognized some of these shadows in yourself or your loved ones, you now know that these issues can be resolved through reflection and communication. The archetypes are merely the mirror of humanity, allowing you to take a closer, impartial look at what makes people tick and why they do certain things. It's an exercise in self-realization and empathy, meant to show you the hidden potential within yourself and everyone around you.

If you enjoyed this book, I'd greatly appreciate a review on Amazon because it helps me to create more books that people want. It would mean a lot to hear from you.

To leave a review:
1. Open your camera app.
2. Point your mobile device at the QR code.
3. The review page will appear in your web browser.

Thanks for your support!

Here's another book by Mari Silva that you might like

Your Free Gift
(only available for a limited time)

Thanks for getting this book! If you want to learn more about various spirituality topics, then join Mari Silva's community and get a free guided meditation MP3 for awakening your third eye. This guided meditation mp3 is designed to open and strengthen ones third eye so you can experience a higher state of consciousness. Simply visit the link below the image to get started.

https://spiritualityspot.com/meditation
Or, Scan the QR code!

References

Abogado, I. (2023, December 5). The Lover Archetype. Meaning in Psychology - The Brain Blog. The Brain Blog. https://thebrain.blog/the-lover-archetype/

Alex & Emma. (2025, March 26). The Seeker Archetype: Discovery, Intuition, & Personal Growth. Personality-Type.com | Master Yourself & Win the Game of Life. https://personality-type.com/seeker-archetype

Cherry, K. (2023, March 11). The 4 Major Jungian Archetypes. Verywell Mind. https://www.verywellmind.com/what-are-jungs-4-major-archetypes-2795439

Copley, L. (2024, April 8). 12 Jungian Archetypes: The Foundation of Personality. PositivePsychology.com. https://positivepsychology.com/jungian-archetypes/

Feccomandi, A. (2023, November 21). Trickster Archetype | Who is the Trickster? Examples and Use. Bibisco Blog. https://bibisco.com/blog/trickster-archetype-examples-and-use/

Feccomandi, A. (2023, November 29). Jungian Archetypes | Examples and Overview. Bibisco. https://bibisco.com/blog/jungian-archetypes-examples-and-overview/

Hudnall, A. (2016, May 14). Archetypes: Magician. Ariel Hudnall. https://arielhudnall.com/2016/05/15/archetypes-magician/

Hudnall, A. (2015, December 1). Archetypes: Sage. Ariel Hudnall. https://arielhudnall.com/2015/12/01/archetypes-sage/

Hudnall, A. (2015, June 28). Archetypes: Creator. Ariel Hudnall. https://arielhudnall.com/2015/06/28/archetypes-creator/

Hudnall, A. (2015, March 16). Archetypes: Explorer. Ariel Hudnall. https://arielhudnall.com/2015/03/16/archetypes-explorer/

Hudnall, A. (2015, March 29). Archetypes: Outlaw. Ariel Hudnall. https://arielhudnall.com/2015/03/29/archetypes-outlaw/

Hudnall, A. (2015, March 8). Archetypes: Caregiver. Ariel Hudnall; Ariel Hudnall. https://arielhudnall.com/2015/03/08/archetypes-caregiver/

Hudnall, A. (2015, May 25). Archetypes: Lover. Ariel Hudnall. https://arielhudnall.com/2015/05/25/archetypes-lover/

Hudnall, A. (2015, September 6). Archetypes: Jester. Ariel Hudnall; Ariel Hudnall. https://arielhudnall.com/2015/09/06/archetypes-jester/

Jeffrey, S. (2017, May 15). Archetypes: A Practical Guide to Inner Work Using Archetypes. Scott Jeffrey. https://scottjeffrey.com/archetypes-psychology/

Jeffrey, S. (2018, July 5). Magician Archetype: the Knower and the Creator of Worlds. Scott Jeffrey. https://scottjeffrey.com/magician-archetype/

Know Your Archetypes. (n.d.). Innocent Archetype. Know Your Archetypes. https://knowyourarchetypes.com/archetype-personality-types/innocent-archetype/

KnowYourArchetypes. (2020, June 23). What is the Warrior Archetype? (Characteristics + Examples). Know Your Archetypes. https://knowyourarchetypes.com/warrior-archetype/

KnowYourArchetypes. (n.d.). Hero Archetype. Know Your Archetypes. https://knowyourarchetypes.com/archetype-personality-types/hero-archetype/

Landsborough, D. (2022, February 10). The Sage Archetype - Everything You Need To Know. Www.dabblewriter.com. https://www.dabblewriter.com/articles/the-sage-archetype

Landsborough, D. (2022a, January 27). The Magician Archetype - Everything You Need to Know. Www.dabblewriter.com. https://www.dabblewriter.com/articles/the-magician-archetype

Landsborough, D. (2022b, February 22). The Creator Archetype - Everything You Need to Know. Www.dabblewriter.com. https://www.dabblewriter.com/articles/the-creator-archetype

Leighfield, L. (2023, November 7). The 12 Character Archetypes | Boords. Boords.com. https://boords.com/storytelling/character-archetypes#1-the-innocent

Neill, C. (2018, April 21). Understanding personality: The 12 Jungian Archetypes. Moving People to Action. https://conorneill.com/2018/04/21/understanding-personality-the-12-jungian-archetypes/

Sebastian, E. (2023, December 28). Understanding the Hero Archetype: A Psychological View. Medium. https://medium.com/@Beyond-A.I./understanding-the-hero-archetype-a-psychological-view-e542bbd7c92d

Tuli, N. (2022, February 1). The Lover Archetype - Everything You Need To Know. Www.dabblewriter.com. https://www.dabblewriter.com/articles/the-lover-archetype

Tuli, N. (2022, February 8). The Explorer Archetype - Everything You Need To Know. Www.dabblewriter.com. https://www.dabblewriter.com/articles/the-explorer-archetype

Tuli, N. (2022, March 3). The Outlaw Archetype – Everything You Need To Know. Www.dabblewriter.com. https://www.dabblewriter.com/articles/the-outlaw-archetype-everything-you-need-to-know

Wurdeman, A. (2022, February 15). The Innocent Archetype – Everything You Need to Know. Www.dabblewriter.com. https://www.dabblewriter.com/articles/the-innocent-archetype

Wurdeman, A. (2022, February 24). The Caregiver Archetype - Everything You Need to Know. Www.dabblewriter.com. https://www.dabblewriter.com/articles/the-caregiver-archetype-everything-you-need-to-know

Wurdeman, A. (2022, February 3). The Jester Archetype - Everything You Need to Know. Www.dabblewriter.com. https://www.dabblewriter.com/articles/the-jester-archetype

Wurdeman, A. (2022, January 25). The Hero Archetype - Everything You Need To Know. Www.dabblewriter.com. https://www.dabblewriter.com/articles/the-hero-archetype

Yuan, L. (2022, January 3). Guide: 12 Jungian Archetypes as Popularized by The Hero and the Outlaw | Personality Psychology. Medium; Personality Psychology. https://medium.com/personalitypsychology/guide-12-jungian-archetypes-as-popularized-by-the-hero-and-the-outlaw-6acd5c6888be

Image Sources

1 Photo by ShotPot: https://www.pexels.com/photo/reflection-of-a-woman-on-a-mirror-6337335/
2 https://commons.wikimedia.org/wiki/File:ETH-BIB-Jung,_Carl_Gustav_(1875-1961)-Portrait-Portr_14163_(cropped).tif
3 https://commons.wikimedia.org/wiki/File:Plato-raphael.jpg
4 Photo by Rene Terp: https://www.pexels.com/photo/little-girl-with-10970526/
5 Photo by Helena Lopes: https://www.pexels.com/photo/men-s-white-button-up-dress-shirt-708440/
6 Designed by jcomp at Freepik. https://www.freepik.com/free-photo/girl-with-arms-streched-colored-balloons_907970.htm#fromView=search&page=2&position=24&uuid=5eac9a54-b5a4-456f-a3ef-8803c75442fc&query=inner+child
7 Designed by jcomp at Freepik. https://www.freepik.com/free-photo/silhouette-top-mountain-is-successful_6172110.htm#fromView=search&page=1&position=4&uuid=88767202-d1e3-4850-a007-19fa6876c18f&query=survivor
8 Photo by Eugene Golovesov: https://www.pexels.com/photo/birds-flying-under-a-pink-sky-5097165/
9 Photo by Philip Ackermann : https://www.pexels.com/photo/person-running-near-street-between-tall-trees-878151/
10 Photo by Heriberto Jahir Medina: https://www.pexels.com/photo/woman-in-a-black-tank-top-holding-a-weapon-7700348/
11 Photo by Pavel Danilyuk: https://www.pexels.com/photo/themis-figurine-at-lawyers-office-8112199/
12 Photo by Pixabay: https://www.pexels.com/photo/person-holding-white-flower-460295/

13 Photo by Jasmin Wedding Photography: https://www.pexels.com/photo/man-and-woman-near-grass-field-1415131/
14 Photo by Valentin Antonucci: https://www.pexels.com/photo/person-holding-compass-841286/
15 Photo by Dó Castle: https://www.pexels.com/photo/man-sitting-beside-bicycle-2270328/
16 Photo by Nils Lindner on Unsplash https://unsplash.com/photos/black-and-white-brick-wall-gjDUz4wQnxs
17 Photo by Pavel Danilyuk: https://www.pexels.com/photo/woman-in-red-long-sleeve-shirt-8638231/
18 Photo by Designecologist: https://www.pexels.com/photo/heart-shaped-red-neon-signage-887349/
19 Photo by Ron Lach : https://www.pexels.com/photo/a-woman-in-white-top-holding-a-crystal-ball-8262602/
20 Photo by Brett Sayles: https://www.pexels.com/photo/photo-of-woman-painting-on-wall-1340502/
21 Photo by Pixabay: https://www.pexels.com/photo/low-section-of-man-against-sky-247851/
22 Photo by Pavel Danilyuk: https://www.pexels.com/photo/a-man-in-deep-thoughts-8438920/
23 Photo by Pixabay: https://www.pexels.com/photo/eyeglasses-on-an-opened-book-267582/

www.ingramcontent.com/pod-product-compliance
Lightning Source LLC
Chambersburg PA
CBHW072152200426
43209CB00052B/1158